Gluten-free, Wheat-free, Dairy-free & Refined Sugar-free

CHRISTMAS TREATS FROM AROUND THE WORLD

By Eva Detko, PhD

Get more recipes and updates at:

www.dr-eva.com

CONTENTS

From the author

I guess out of all the special occasions, Christmas can be the trickiest. There is a lot of pressure on people to deliver amazing food and this pressure can increase exponentially when you have to cater for people with special dietary requirements. Many people end up cooking separately for those on special diets. Of course, the efforts are very much appreciated but the bottom line is that the host ends up with much more work, and therefore stress, and the "special" guests feel different or a burden. In the case of the host having a restricted diet, I often hear them being concerned as to whether the guests are going to like their food. Or again, they cook separately for their guests. But it does not have to be this way. My guests always eat wheat, gluten, dairy and refined sugar-free food, and they love it. In fact, I have converted a few people to gluten and dairy-free lifestyles.

When I released my first cook book at the end of November last year, naturally many people wanted to know if the book contained any recipes to get them through Christmas. As a result, I promised to put together a book of recipes that would hit the Christmas spot. As most people find Christmas baking more challenging than making the main meal, I decided to focus on some classic Christmas desserts and make them as close to the original recipes as possible. Of course, using gluten-free flour and not using refined sugar means that the taste and texture cannot always be exactly the same, but I worked hard to make sure that those recipes really do taste great, despite being gluten-free and low in sugar. I then thought, what about including some of the great Polish Christmas classics I grew up with? And that is how the Christmas treats from around the world idea was born. I also wanted to make sure there is plenty in this book for both adults and children to enjoy.

Before you say: "I am not that good in the kitchen", these recipes are designed so that the novice cooks can follow them. So please, give it ago as you may be very pleasantly surprised with the outcome. Even though, the availability of free-from food is much greater now than it was 16 years ago, when I first discovered I could not eat gluten, bought food will never come even remotely close to what you can make yourself.

I am very excited to bring you this new cook book as I am hoping you will enjoy these recipes as much as I did enjoy creating them.

Have a magical Christmas!

Acknowledgments

Dedicated to my wonderful grandma (1929-2013), an inspirational lady who made the best apple pie in the world.

I will always cherish the memories of us baking together.

Thank you for this amazing gift.

A massive thank you to my amazing partner Pete. Thank you for always being there for me, motivating me thorough the difficult times, and celebrating my successes.

A special thank you to my mum for continuously supporting me in everything I embark on and for providing inspiration for my culinary experiments.

Thank you to Nigel Wilson of Love Vintage Settings in Chippenham for kindly letting me use his beautiful china that gives the photos the true Christmas feel.

I would also like to thank Cathy and Andy Thatcher, and Andrea Dell, for rummaging through their lofts looking for Christmas decorations in the middle of the summer.

Big thanks to our friend, Adam Davidson, for trusting us with his photographic equipment.

Last but most certainly not least, thank you to both our families, and friends, for sampling the recipes and providing valuable feedback.

Guide to symbols

 Low calorie content
(250 calories or less per serving)

 Very low sugar content
(no more than 10% of calories coming from sugar)

 Good source of fibre
(at least 5 grams per serving)

 Low estimated glycaemic load (10 or less); note that this is an estimate (refer to section: Understanding glycaemic index and glycaemic load for more information)

 Quick to prepare (30 min or less preparation time)

 Suitable for freezing (it is recommended to portion before freezing and consume within 3 months; once defrosted, consume the same day)

 Best eaten straight away as does not keep or freeze well

Weights and conversions

Measurements:

- Both imperial and metric measurements are provided in each recipe.
- It is recommended to be consistent with the type of measurements used.
- Nutritional analysis for each recipe is based on metric measurements.
- Conversions to imperial units are approximate (rounded up or down to the nearest 0.5 oz or fl oz). This means that if this is your preferred method of measurement, you should remember that the nutritional information will not be as accurate as it would be if metric measurements were used.
- Tablespoon (tbs) and teaspoon (tsp) measurements used in the recipes are level. Due to differences in spoon sizes, cooks in Australia are advised to use 3 level teaspoons for every tablespoon listed in a recipe.
- Those wishing to use cups are advised to use cup measurements for liquid ingredients only. Even though I provided some approximate cup measurements for solid ingredients, it is recommended to use kitchen scales to measure those more accurately.
- Egg sizes specified in the recipes refer to the UK (and European) egg sizes (small: less than 53 g; medium: 53-63 g; large: 63-73 g). Note that egg sizes in the US, Australia and Canada are different. For example, medium egg in the US weighs: 50-57 g, in Canada: 49-55 g, and in Australia: 42-50 g.

Oven temperatures:

Gas mark	ºC	ºC Fan	ºF	Temperature
0.5	120	100	250	very cool
1	140	120	275	cool
2	150	130	300	cool
3	160	140	325	warm
4	180	160	350	moderate
5	190	170	375	moderately hot
6	200	180	400	fairly hot
7	220	200	425	hot
8	230	210	450	very hot
9	240	220	475	very hot

Liquid conversions:

Note that these conversions are approximates.

US	Australia	Metric	Imperial
0.25 cup	0.25 cup	60 ml	2 fl oz
0.5 cup	0.5 cup	120 ml	4 fl oz
0.75 cup	0.75 cup	180 ml	6 fl oz
1 cup	1 cup	235 ml	8 fl oz
2 cups / 1 pint	2 cups	475 ml	16 fl oz
2.5 cups	1 pint	590 ml	20 fl oz
3 cups	1.25 pints	710 ml	24 fl oz
3.5 cups	1.5 pints	830 ml	28 fl oz
4 cups / 1 quart	1.75 pints	950 ml	32 fl oz

Solid conversions:

Note that these conversions are approximates (rounded up / down to the nearest 5 g).

Ingredient	1 cup	3/4 cup	2/3 cup	1/2 cup	1/3 cup	1/4 cup
Almond flakes	80 g	60 g	55 g	40 g	25 g	20 g
Amaranth (uncooked)	195 g	145 g	130 g	95 g	65 g	50 g
Creamed coconut / cacao paste / cacao butter / (small chunks)	235 g	175 g	155 g	120 g	80 g	60 g
Cherries	155 g	115 g	105 g	80 g	50 g	40 g
Cooked chestnuts	130 g	100 g	85 g	65 g	45 g	35 g
Desiccated coconut	100 g	75 g	65 g	50 g	35 g	25 g
Flour	120 g	90 g	80 g	60 g	40 g	30 g
Nuts (chopped)	150 g	110 g	100 g	75 g	50 g	40 g
Nuts (ground) / milled flax seed	120 g	90 g	80 g	60 g	40 g	30 g
Peach slices / pear slices	225 g	170 g	150 g	115 g	75 g	55 g
Pineapple chunks	180 g	135 g	120 g	90 g	60 g	45 g
Poppy seeds	135 g	100 g	90 g	70 g	45 g	35 g
Pumpkin puree	245 g	185 g	165 g	125 g	80 g	60 g
Raisins / sultanas / mixed dried fruit / dried cranberries	200 g	150 g	130 g	100 g	65 g	50 g
Ready-to-eat dried prunes / dates / apricots / mango (finely chopped)	180 g	135 g	120 g	90 g	60 g	45 g
Sweetcorn (tinned, drained)	165 g	125 g	110 g	80 g	55 g	40 g
Sweet potato (raw, diced)	135 g	100 g	90 g	70 g	45 g	35 g

If you react to wheat or gluten

All the recipes in this book are both wheat and gluten-free (to read my blog about the differences between wheat and gluten, go to: *www.dr-eva.com/what-is-the-difference-between-wheat-free-and-gluten-free*). Please note that there are different flour mixes available on the market. If you have coeliac disease, dermatitis herpetiformis, or are otherwise sensitive gluten, you should only buy ingredients and foods that are certified "gluten-free". If you have a wheat allergy, you should ensure everything you buy is labeled "wheat-free", as gluten-free products often contain wheat flour from which gluten has been removed. The example of that are Glutafin gluten-free flour mixes and products. Glutafin flour mixes contain gluten-free wheat starch and rather disgustingly: sugar, dried glucose syrup, and skimmed milk powder.

If you wish to use regular dairy products, rather than the offered dairy-free alternatives, feel free to do so but be aware that the nutritional information (including: sugar, fat, calorie content, and estimated glycaemic load information) may change, depending on the alternative used. If you decide to use regular dairy products, I recommend going for the reduced-fat options. I also recommend reducing the overall amount of dairy you consume (to read my blog "Dairy - 10 good reasons to give a wide berth", go to: *www.dr-eva.com/dairy-10-good-reasons-to-give-it-a-wide-berth*).

If you react to dairy or lactose

All the recipes in this book are dairy-free. If you react to dairy or lactose and do not seem to react to wheat or gluten, I would still encourage you to consider the wheat-free / gluten-free alternatives offered in this book (to read my blog "Wheat and gluten: 10 good reasons to avoid them", go to: *www.dr-eva.com/wheat-and-gluten-10-good-reasons-to-avoid-them*).

If you are lactose-intolerant, you may choose to use lactose-free ingredients in place of the dairy-free alternatives offered. Be aware however, that this may affect the nutritional analysis provided, and does not resolve the issue of dairy being pro-inflammatory, and full of contaminants.

If you are a vegetarian

All the recipes in this book are vegetarian. Four of the recipes require the use of gelatine but a vegetarian / vegan alternative can be used.

If you react to eggs or do not wish to eat them

11 recipes in this book are naturally egg-free. The remaining recipes do call for eggs, however in the majority of these egg replacers can be used. For more information on which egg replacers to use and how they affect the nutritional information, refer to section *Egg replacers* on page 14.

If you react to soya or do not wish to eat it

All of the recipes in this book are dairy-free and soya-free at the same time.

If you have diabetes

The nutritional information provided with each recipe enables you to track how much carbohydrate you eat, and therefore helps you keep your blood glucose levels within your target range. In order to help you achieve that, the nutritional information provided with each recipe includes: 1) the amount of carbohydrates in grams; 2) the number of carbohydrate portions (CPs), or carbohydrate exchanges; and 3) the estimated glycaemic load (GL) value (refer to section Understanding glycaemic index and glycaemic load on page 16 for more information).

Please note that in this book, as accepted in the UK, one CP is equal to 10 g of carbohydrate. This is different to the equivalents in the US and Australia, where one CP is equal to 15 g of carbohydrate. The CPs in this book are adjusted for fibre content. This means that where the fibre content per serving was 5 g or more, the number of CPs per serving was calculated by subtracting half of the fibre content from the total carbohydrate content and divided by 10.

As for the GL, it is typically recommended to aim for 100 or less per day. However, some experts agree that people with diabetes should aim even lower. All the treats included in this book have low to moderate GL values (ranging from 0.2 to 19 per serving). Please note, that the GL values are estimates and should be used for guideline purposes only. If you have diabetes (particularly, if it is insulin-dependent), you should not rely solely on the GL information. It is best to have a range of tools that help you monitor your carbohydrate intake. The amount of carbohydrate that is right for you depends on many things, including how active you are and what, if any, medicines you take. Seek advice of a medical practitioner if you are unsure how much carbohydrate you should consume and what method of carbohydrate monitoring may be right for you. The important thing is to have a dietary strategy tailored to your lifestyle that helps you achieve your goals for: blood glucose, blood lipids (fats), blood pressure, and weight management. It is also important that you read information in section Stevia and other sugar substitutes on page 15 before you start using the recipes in this book.

If you do not want to use stevia

Stevia is a natural sugar substitute (plant extract) that I use in all my sweet recipes (more information about stevia in section Stevia and other sugar substitutes on page 15). The recipes in this book specify the number of stevia servings. As stevia is much sweeter than sugar, one serving is a very small amount (usually ⅛ of a teaspoon if it is powdered, or 4-5 drops if is in a liquid form). I have found that with most pure stevia extracts, one serving is an equivalent of 1 level teaspoon of sugar (5 grams). I cannot guarantee that this is the case for every single stevia brand out there but does apply to brands, such as: SweetLeaf, NOW, and Natures Way. If you do not wish to use stevia, you can just supplement the stevia in the sweet recipes with other sugar substitutes (e.g. xylitol, agave or rice syrup), or sugar. To substitute stevia for sugar, just multiply the number of stevia servings specified in the recipe by five to find out how many grams of sugar to add.

Some other things you should know before you start using this book

Ingredients

The majority of ingredients used in the recipes in this book can be bought in most supermarkets. This includes many wheat, gluten, and dairy-free ingredients, such as: gluten-free flour, coconut oil, xanthan gum, creamed coconut, coconut cream, as well as almond, rice and coconut milk.

A very small number of ingredients used in this book (e.g. stevia, cacao paste, cacao butter) may not be available in your local supermarket. However, those ingredients are readily available online, or from health food shops, and tend to have a reasonably long shelf-life.

Wheat and gluten substitutes

As mentioned previously, there are many substitutes for gluten-containing grains (i.e. wheat, rye and barley). Commonly available gluten-free flour blends are usually a mixture of rice, tapioca, potato, corn, and / or buckwheat flour. You can also buy those flours on their own, but some gluten-free flours take some getting used to in terms of their taste and texture. For example, many people find that white rice flour has a gummy taste to it, which is the reason why I do not use it on its own. I find that flour blends taste more neutral (I tend to use Doves Farm flour, or mix my own). They work well in most recipes and are better than single flours when used for baking, due to combining different relative flour weights. If you have a wheat allergy, you should be aware that certain gluten-free flour mixes (e.g. Glutafin) contain wheat starch from which gluten has been removed. Therefore, you should ensure that everything you buy is labeled "wheat-free". Either way, it is recommended to read labels when buying flour mixes as they may also contain other ingredients you wish to avoid, e.g. sugar, dried glucose syrup, skimmed milk powder, etc. (Glutafin again).

Apart from the substitutes already mentioned, there are many other types of gluten-free flour, including: quinoa, amaranth, almond, hazelnut, coconut, teff, carob, millet, chickpea, soya, sorghum (also known as jowar flour), and gluten-free oat flour. If flour blends available in shops are not to your taste, you can always try mixing your own blend. However, be aware that gluten-free flours have different tastes, and their texture dictates how they behave in a recipe. For example, coconut flour is rich in fibre and requires adding extra liquid to a recipe. Sorghum flour adds sweetness to recipes. Some flours should be approached with caution. This includes legume-based flours, such as soya and chickpea flour. Some people with coeliac disease may not tolerate them well. In addition to that, excessive consumption of soya should be avoided due to high levels of lectins, phyto-oeastrogens, and other undesirable compounds it contains. It is also worth noting that there have been reports of high levels of arsenic in brown rice flour.

As for oat flour, clinical evidence confirms that most people with coeliac disease, dermatitis herpetiformis, wheat allergy, and non-coeliac gluten sensitivity can safely consume moderate amounts of pure oats. This is the general consensus in the UK and the rest of Europe, as well as in the US and Canada. However, coeliac associations in Australia and New Zealand still advise coeliac sufferers not to consume oats at all. Just to clarify, pure oats are actually gluten-free.

However, oats found on supermarket shelves tend to be cross-contaminated with other gluten-containing grains. Therefore, should you choose to use oat flour ensure that it is certified "gluten-free". A very small number of coeliac sufferers will react to a different protein in oats called avenin. If you are amongst those who react to avenin, you should avoid products containing oats and oat flour.

Commonly available self-raising flour mixes tend to contain binding components (e.g. xanthan gum or guar gum) and leavening agents (e.g. sodium bicarbonate, monocalcium phosphate). Adding these helps improve texture of gluten-free baked goods. It is gluten that makes regular baked goods fluffy by making dough "stretchy" and helping goods rise. Gluten-free flours do not have the same "stretchy" capacity but adding binding and leavening agents can help improve the quality of gluten-free baking. However, I do not believe that adding gums is essential to every single gluten-free recipe. In fact, adding too much of these ingredients can promote heavy, "gummy" texture. It is also worth noting that xanthan gum tends to be derived from corn so may not be suitable for those with corn sensitivity. Guar gum is legume-derived, so those sensitive to legumes (including soya) may react to it. If you need to avoid using gums, try using one tablespoon of arrowroot, potato or tapioca starch mixed with a few tablespoons of warm water. Ground flax seed can also work well in some recipes.

When it comes to baking powder, not all baking powders are gluten-free so ensure that it states "gluten-free" on the label. You should also make sure that the baking powder you buy is free of aluminium (check the label for sodium aluminium sulphate, or SAS). Baking powder is not the same as baking soda (sodium bicarbonate), even though it contains baking soda. Baking soda needs an acidic ingredient (e.g. vinegar, molasses, honey, maple syrup or lemon juice) to start the gas-releasing process that gives baked goods their rise. If a recipe does not contain an acidic ingredient, baking soda will not work. On the other hand, baking powder will, as it contains both the alkaline and acidic ingredients.

For anybody who would like to mix their own flour, here is an example of a flour blend that works well in baked goods: a mixture of equal parts (100 g / 4 oz) of sorghum, oat (or almond) and quinoa flour, combined with 200 g (7 oz) of potato starch (not potato flour), 1 teaspoon of gluten and aluminium-free baking powder, and 1 teaspoon of xanthan gum (or preferred alternative).

Please note that the nutritional analysis of the recipes is based on a standard flour mix readily available in supermarkets. Using flours with a higher fat content, e.g. coconut or almond flour will alter the nutritional information.

Dairy substitutes

I find that replacing dairy in recipes is a bit more challenging than replacing wheat or gluten. This is particularly true if you want to minimize the use of soya. Soya contains phyto-oeastrogens (mimic human oeastrogens), phytates, lectins, saponins, goitrogens, as well as many contaminants (unless bought organic). Consuming excessive amounts of soya may result in malabsorption of vital nutrients, weight gain, digestive, immune and fertility problems. Fermented soya products (e.g. yoghurt, miso, tempeh) are more acceptable as fermentation deactivates many undesirable compounds, but should be still consumed in moderation. The bottom line is that soya is not as good for your health as it was once believed, and therefore I only use it sparingly. In fact, all of the recipes in this book are soya-free.

When it comes to substituting milk, there are many alternatives other than soya, including: rice, almond, hazelnut, and coconut milk. I recommend buying the unsweetened versions. All of those milk substitutes can be bought in most supermarkets. Coconut milk is available as "regular" or "light" (lower fat content), and you can also buy it organic. Coconut milk works very well in both sweet and savoury dishes, and is excellent for baking. Some milk substitutes may take some getting used to, but try them a few times, and in different dishes, to give your taste buds an opportunity to adjust to these new flavours. If you are lactose intolerant you may be fine using milk and milk products to which enzyme lactase has been added.

You may also be able to tolerate small amounts of goat's or sheep's milk. Substituting cream in recipes is also relatively simple. Non-soya, dairy-free alternatives include rice and coconut cream. If you decide to use soya cream, note that not all soya cream is gluten-free so check the label.

When it comes to substituting butter, my personal preferences are coconut oil and creamed coconut (fresh coconut sold in the form of white solid block, which is different from coconut cream), as they work very well in baked goods. Coconut oil is very heat stable and has many health benefits. Some people choose to use lard, which used to be considered "evil" but is now making a come-back. As it happens, lard is far better from the health and flavour perspective compared to any margarine (hydrogenated / solidified vegetable fat), which is really damaging to our health.

Egg replacers

I would encourage you to source a neutral "free-from" egg replacer that you can use in both sweet and savoury dishes. Orgran and Energ-G egg replacers are starch-based (potato and tapioca) and free from wheat, dairy, gluten, egg, yeast and soya. To make your own egg replacer, use 1 tablespoon of tapioca or potato starch mixed with 3 tablespoons of water for each egg in a recipe. The difference in taste when using egg replacers is detectable, but not overwhelming or unpleasant in any way. Using these egg replacers in baked goods tends to make them slightly denser, so you may want to increase leavening to compensate for that, e.g. add additional quarter of a teaspoon of baking powder. If you choose to use egg replacers, it is best to go for flour blends that do not contain tapioca, as too much tapioca will give your baked goods hardness that may not be desirable.

The energy content of egg replacers is much lower than eggs (on average 10 to 20 calories per serving). Egg replacers contain no fat, cholesterol or protein. However, because most egg replacers are starch-based, unlike eggs, they contain carbohydrates. This means that the estimated GL of the recipe will increase (on average by 1.5 per every egg replacer). If you wish to calculate the GL increase per serving in a given recipe, you need to multiply the number of egg replacers by 1.5 and divide by the number of servings.

Stevia and other sugar substitutes

Stevia is a plant that is native to South America, where it has been used for hundreds of years. Stevia works well for both, non-baked and baked recipes. The two sweetening components identified in stevia are stevioside and rebaudioside A. They are considered safe when used as sweetening agents in foods and are a much better option than any artificial sweeteners (e.g. aspartame, acesulfame K, or saccharin). I also prefer stevia over xylitol (often used in sugar-free products), as xylitol gives me stomach pain and sends my bowel into a frenzy. On the other hand, I have used stevia for a long time and I have never experienced any adverse symptoms as a result of ingesting it. Having said that, I know people who use xylitol in baking with good results and no symptoms.

Recipes in this book do not contain any refined sugar. There are a few recipes that give an option of using icing (or icing sugar) for decoration but this is not essential to the success of the recipe and can be omitted. I choose to use a combination of stevia and honey (which some people will argue is not much different from sugar unless used raw) as in my opinion this produces the best results. I find that using stevia on its own, despite it being a natural sugar substitute, tends to make the taste quite artificial. As usual, I encourage you to exercise moderation. This applies to both, honey and stevia. As long as you have a wide variety of food, and do not just live on cake, I do not see a problem with using either. Moreover, even though the recipes do contain small amounts of honey, they are designed so that the estimated GL value is kept low or moderate. This means that the total sugar content of these recipes is still relatively low.

I would encourage you to source a pure stevia extract, which you can get in the form of drops or powder. There are many products on the market and they tend to vary in potency and taste. The serving size will also vary depending on the brand, and whether it is in liquid or powder form. The recipes in this book specify a number of stevia servings but you may need to adjust that according to personal taste. Please note that stevia-derived products available from supermarkets (e.g. Truvia) are highly processed. Therefore, even though they will not compromise the recipes, I do not recommend using them for health reasons. You may need to experiment with a few before you find the one you like. Brands worth considering include: SweatLeaf, NOW, Natures Way, and Planetary Herbals.

It is worth noting that stevia may have a lowering effect on blood sugar, although the research supporting this is inconclusive. If you have diabetes and wish to use stevia, monitor your blood sugar closely and report your findings to your healthcare provider, as the dose of your diabetes medication might need to be adjusted. There is also some evidence, though also inconclusive, that stevia may lower blood pressure. This may be a consideration for people who have low blood pressure, or are on medication for high blood pressure. Additional considerations when using stevia include: allergy to sunflower and aster plant family (Asteraceae), pregnancy and breast-feeding, and medications containing lithium. Again, check with your healthcare provider if you are unsure if stevia is the right sugar substitute for you. Please be aware that stevia is still one of the safest sugar substitutes on the market. If for whatever reason you do not wish to use stevia, you can replace it with other sweetening agents, but you should bear in mind that some of them (e.g. agave syrup, date sugar, maple syrup, fruit juice concentrate, molasses) do increase blood sugar levels. If you decide to use sugar, multiply the number of stevia servings specified in a given recipe by five. That will give you the number of grams of sugar required for that recipe (1 serving of stevia = 1 teaspoon of sugar = 5 grams of sugar).

Understanding glycaemic index and glycaemic load

When we eat, digestible carbohydrates in our food get converted into blood sugar (glucose). Blood sugar is the body's preferential source of energy. Our blood sugar levels affect how hungry and how energetic we feel. They also determine whether we burn fat or store it. The hormone responsible for transporting excess blood sugar after a meal into our cells is insulin (produced by the pancreas). Another pancreatic hormone called glucagon works in an opposite way.

Glucagon activates the release of glucose into the bloodstream when the blood sugar level is low. When our diet is balanced, these two hormones work well together, successfully maintaining our blood sugar levels within a fairly narrow range. However, when we regularly consume sugary or refined carbohydrate-rich foods, this delicate hormonal balance becomes disrupted. This is because sugary and refined carbohydrate foods are processed and released into the bloodstream quickly. This tends to cause a large increase in blood sugar, which in turn stimulates the pancreas to release a substantial amount of insulin. The release of insulin assists with the removal of excess glucose from the bloodstream. This is an important mechanism, as chronic high blood glucose levels are dangerous and lead to organ damage. Unfortunately, at the same time insulin signals that plenty of energy is readily available in the form of glucose and that the body should stop burning fat and start storing it. As mentioned earlier, glucose is the body's preferential fuel, which means that when glucose is available, the body prefers using it over fat.

To make things even worse, these exaggerated insulin surges can cause too much blood sugar to be transported from the bloodstream into the body's cells. This can result in blood sugar dropping below normal levels, leading to hypoglycaemia (low blood sugar). When this happens, we feel sluggish, irritable and hungry. This is an undesirable state to be in because the brain relies on glucose as its only source of fuel, so the body responds to protect us. As a result, at this point we tend to crave foods high in sugar. Acting on those cravings causes a spike in our blood sugar, quickly followed by a slump in energy levels. This can easily turn into a vicious cycle of temporary "highs", followed by lethargy, sugar cravings, and of course resulting fat storage.

Furthermore, overproduction of insulin, occurring repeatedly over a period of time, may lead to the body's cells starting to ignore insulin (insulin resistance), or the pancreas stopping to produce enough insulin. This can in turn cause excessive build-up of glucose in the bloodstream, leading to the development of type 2 diabetes. Moreover, when the body is unable to effectively use the insulin that is being produced, chronic high insulin levels (hyperinsulinaemia) may result. Hyperinsulinaemia is strongly linked to overweight and obesity, as well as increased risk of heart disease and cancer (in particular colon and breast cancer).

This means that eating foods that "spike" blood sugar quickly and cause repeated exposure to large amounts of insulin is best avoided. This type of eating pattern can result in weight gain (or difficulties losing weight), and other serious health problems (e.g. diabetes, cardiovascular disease, kidney problems). Conclusion: to maintain desirable weight and good health, we need to keep our blood sugar and insulin levels stable. In order to achieve this, we need to be aware of the carbohydrate content of our food, as well as the concept of glycaemic index and glycaemic load.

The glycaemic index, (GI) provides a measure of how quickly blood sugar levels increase after eating a particular type of food. This is important because the effects of different foods on blood sugar levels (glycaemic response) are highly variable. The GI is a ranking of carbohydrate foods on a scale from 0 to 100, according to the extent to which they raise blood sugar levels after eating. This is estimated using pure glucose as a reference, the GI of which has been set at 100. GI values of 55 or less are considered "low," between 56 and 69 are considered "moderate", and above 70 are considered "high." GI values are determined experimentally by feeding human participants a fixed portion of a given food (after an overnight fast), and subsequently measuring their blood glucose response to this food at specific intervals. This process is expensive and time-consuming, and there are only a limited number of laboratories across the world performing these tests. For this reason, GI data is only available for selected foods we consume.

The theory behind the GI is to minimize insulin-related health problems by identifying and avoiding foods that have the greatest impact on blood sugar levels. Before this concept was developed, simple sugars (e.g. table sugar, sweets) had been believed to be digested quickly and cause a rapid increase in blood sugar. On the other hand, "complex carbohydrates" (e.g. bread) had been thought to be processed and released into the bloodstream more slowly. We now know that this is not always the case. While many sweet and sugary foods do have high GI values, some starchy foods (e.g. white bread) have higher GI values than honey or table sugar.

One limitation of the GI is that it does not take into account the amount of carbohydrate actually consumed. This is a problem because the body's glycaemic response is dependent on both the type AND the amount of carbohydrate consumed. This means that you could have a small amount of food with a high GI value (e.g. a couple of jelly beans) and your glycaemic response will be relatively small. Conversely, you could have a large amount of food that has a much lower GI value (e.g. potato chips) and produce a much higher glycaemic response. To correct for that, the concept of glycaemic load (GL) was developed. GL is calculated in a following way:

GL = GI / 100 x net carbohydrate content
(net carbohydrate content is equal to the total carbohydrate content minus dietary fibre)

GL estimates the impact of carbohydrate consumption using GI values while taking into account the amount of carbohydrate consumed. Generally, GL values below 10 are considered "low," between 10 and 19 are considered "moderate", and above 20 are considered "high." For weight loss and general health, it is recommended to choose low to medium-GI and GL foods in order to in order to keep blood sugar and insulin stable. Most experts recommend that the total GL should be 100 or less per day. People with diabetes or metabolic syndrome might want to aim even lower than this. A number of studies have shown that people on high-GI (high-GL) diets are much more likely to develop type 2 diabetes, age-related macular degeneration, cardiovascular and kidney disease, compared to those on low-GI (low-GL) diets. For people who are physically active and not overweight, daily GL slightly higher than 100 is acceptable.

It is important to remember that glycaemic response varies between individuals and can even vary in the same person from day to day, or from one time of day to another. In addition to that, people can have different insulin responses (i.e. produce different levels of insulin), even with an identical glycaemic response. This means that people who have diabetes cannot rely solely on the GI of foods (or any other food index) without monitoring their own blood sugar response. Moreover, most of the available GI values show the effect of a particular food on glucose levels in the first two hours following ingestion. Some people with diabetes may have elevated blood sugar levels for longer than that.

The nutritional information provided in this book comes from The Composition of Foods (compiled by the UK Foods Standards Agency and Institute of Food Research), additionally supplemented by the information obtained from the Nutrition Data database (based on USDA's National Nutrient Database for Standard Reference). The GL calculations for each recipe in this book are based on the Estimated Glycaemic Load™ (eGL) obtained from the Nutrition Data database. Nutrition Data used a mathematical formula that enabled a comparison between actual and estimated Glycemic Loads for 221 common carbohydrate-containing foods (*http://nutritiondata.self.com/help/estimated-glycemic-load*). Data from *International table of glycaemic index and glycaemic load values: 2002* (Am J Clin Nutr, 76(1):5-56) was utilized in this analysis. The purpose of this was to produce a reasonable estimate for foods for which GI was previously unknown. Even though those eGL values are only estimates, they enable us taking into account foods, which would otherwise have to be ignored due to lack of data.

Please note that the GL values provided in this book are for guideline purposes only. In order to obtain very accurate GL values, each recipe would have to be submitted for the previously described laboratory tests, which would be both extremely expensive and highly impractical. In summary, with all their limitations, the concept of the GI and GL is far from being an exact science. Nonetheless, it is still one of the best tools available in terms of providing information about the impact of carbohydrates on blood sugar levels. This makes it useful when considered alongside other healthy eating tools.

Helpful gadgets

If you are a cooking / baking enthusiast, you probably already have some, if not all, of these items. However, if you are only just starting to discover how much fun making your own food can be, I would really encourage you to invest in the following utensils, as they are both inexpensive and great timesavers: kitchen scales, measuring jug, electric hand whisk, immersion blender, and electric grinder (ideal for grinding nuts, spices, etc.).

RECIPES

POPPY SEED CAKE ROLL

Total Time: 2 hours 55 minutes (preparation only: 30 minutes); Yield: 10 slices

This cake is a popular Christmas treat in many countries of Central and Eastern Europe, including Poland, Hungary, Russia, Slovakia and Croatia.

*One slice contains: Calories: **299** Total Carbohydrate (g): **26** Sugar (g): **6** Carbohydrate Portions: **2.5** Protein (g): **8** Fat (g): **19** Cholesterol (mg): **106** Fibre (g): **5** Glycaemic Load: **15***

Dough: 200 g (7 oz) self-raising gluten-free flour; 50 g (2 oz) golden flax seed (milled); 3 large eggs; 60 ml (2 fl oz) coconut oil; 1 sachet fast-acting dry yeast (2 tsp / 7 g / ¼ oz); 1 tbs runny honey; 1 tsp xanthan gum (or preferred alternative); 30 servings stevia; pinch of salt

Filling: 100g (3½ oz) poppy seeds; 30 g (1 oz) mixed dried fruit; 50 g (2 oz) ground hazelnuts; 50 ml (2 fl oz) unsweetened almond milk; 1 tbs coconut oil; 1 tbs runny honey; 1 large egg; 30 servings stevia; grated zest of a large orange

Additional: greaseproof paper

Method:
1. Soak poppy seeds in hot water for a few hours (or overnight).
2. Put the oven on the lowest setting for 10 minutes while preparing the dough.
3. Mix the dry dough ingredients together, add the wet ingredients (melt coconut oil on low heat first), combine and knead the dough for a few minutes until smooth.
4. Form the dough into a ball, place in an oven-proof dish, cover with cling film and leave in the warm oven to rise (turn the oven off at this point) for approximately 2 hours. The dough should have more or less doubled in size.
5. For the filling, heat up almond milk, add poppy seeds and simmer for few minutes on very low heat.
6. Take the filling mixture off the heat, add the remaining ingredients (separate the egg and leave the white for brushing), combine thoroughly and leave to cool.
7. Once the dough has risen, roll it out on a sheet of greaseproof paper, forming a 30 x 20 cm rectangle (12 x 8 in).
8. Spread the filling evenly, leaving 2 cm (approx. 1 in) off each end.
9. Roll slowly (the longer side) using the paper to help, pinch the ends together so that no filling is visible, transfer onto a non-stick baking tray, and brush with the beaten egg white.
10. Bake in a pre-heated oven at gas mark 5 (190°C / 375°F) for approx. 30-35 minutes (until golden brown).
11. Once cool, cut into 10 slices and consume within 2-3 days (store in an air-tight container), or freeze.

MINCE PIES

Total Time: 1 hour 10 minutes (preparation only: 30-35 minutes); Yield: 12 pies

---

The ingredients of this traditional British Christmas treat can be traced to the 13th century, when returning European crusaders bought with them Middle Eastern recipes containing meats, fruits and spices.

One pie contains: *Calories: **182** Total Carbohydrate (g): **28** Sugar (g): **12** Carbohydrate Portions: **3** Protein (g): **2** Fat (g): **7** Cholesterol (mg): **0** Fibre (g): **2** Glycaemic Load: **17***

<u>Pastry:</u> 200 g (7 oz) self-raising gluten-free flour; 1 large egg; 50 ml (2 fl oz) coconut oil; 1 tbs runny honey; pinch of salt; 8 servings stevia; 6 tbs water

<u>Mincemeat:</u> 150 g (5½ oz) mixed dried fruit; 1 Bramley apple (peeled and grated); 30 ml (1 fl oz) coconut oil; 1 tbs runny honey; 2 tbs brandy (optional); 1 tsp ground cinnamon; 1 tsp allspice; ½ tsp ground cloves; ¼ tsp ground nutmeg; 20 servings stevia; grated zest of a large orange

<u>Additional:</u> sunflower oil spray; dusting of flour

Method:

1. To make the mincemeat, mix all the mincemeat ingredients thoroughly (it is recommended to make your mincemeat a few days or even weeks in advance to give the flavours time to work well together but this is not essential to the success of this recipe).
2. Pre-heat oven to gas mark 5 (190°C / 375°F).
3. To make the pastry combine all the pastry ingredients thoroughly (leave a bit of the egg for brushing), knead for a few minutes (add water gradually as you may need slightly more or slightly less depending on the type of flour you are using), and refrigerate for 10 minutes.
4. Roll out the pastry thinly on a non-stick surface (use a dusting of flour if needed), cut out 12 circles (approx. 6½ cm in diameter / 2½ in), and place in a muffin tray (for small size muffins) coated with sunflower spray and a dusting of flour.
5. Prick the bases of the circles with a fork and blind bake for 7-8 minutes.
6. Remove from the oven and fill with mincemeat.
7. Use the rest of the pastry to cover the mincemeat (cut out stars or other shapes) and brush with rest of the egg (beaten). Bake the pies for 15-20 minutes until golden-brown and serve on their own, or with vanilla sauce (for recipe see GERMAN-STYLE BAKED APPLES WITH VANILLA SAUCE on page 47).
8. Consume within 48 hours (store in an air-tight container), or freeze.

CHOCOLATE & COFFEE BUNDT CAKE

Total Time: 1 hour 15 minutes (preparation only: 15 minutes); Yield: 10 slices

There are endless variations of Bundt cake across the world so why not chocolate & coffee? In some countries Bundt cake is eaten predominantly at Christmas but it can of course be enjoyed all year round.

One slice contains: *Calories:* **237** *Total Carbohydrate (g):* **29** *Sugar (g):* **4** *Carbohydrate Portions:* **3**
Protein (g): **6** *Fat (g):* **11** *Cholesterol (mg):* **114** *Fibre (g):* **2** *Glycaemic Load:* **18**

Cake: 280 g (10 oz) self-raising gluten-free flour; 70 ml (2½ fl oz) coconut oil; 5 med eggs; 250 (9 fl oz) rice milk original; 4 tbs reduced-fat cocoa powder; 2 tbs runny honey; 2 tbs vanilla extract; 3 tsp instant coffee (diluted in 30 ml water) or 3 tsp strong espresso; 1 tsp gluten-free baking powder; 70 servings stevia

Additional: sunflower oil spray; dusting of flour; dusting of icing sugar (optional)

Method:
1. Pre-heat the oven to gas mark 4 (180°C / 350°F).
2. Combine flour with egg yolks, rice milk, honey, coconut oil (melted on low heat), baking powder, and stevia (whisk or stir until smooth but be careful not to overwork the mixture).
3. Beat egg whites to soft peaks and very gently fold into the mixture.
4. Divide the mixture in half, and add vanilla to one part and cocoa powder and coffee to the other (mix in gently).
5. Coat your baking tin with oil spray and a dusting of flour.
6. Transfer the chocolate part of the mixture into the tin, then gently top with the vanilla mixture (for marble effect use a knife and give the mixture a few small stirs being careful not to blend it too much).
7. Bake for 55-60 minutes (until a skewer inserted in the centre of the cake comes out clean).
8. Allow to cool, remove the cake onto a serving tray so it is upside down with the chocolate layer on top, sprinkle with icing sugar (optional), and cut into 10 slices.
9. Consume within 48 hours (store in an air-tight container), or freeze.

BROA CASTELAR (SWEET POTATO COOKIES)

Total Time: 50-55 minutes (preparation only: 25-30 minutes); Yield: 24 cookies

These cookies are a very popular Christmas treat in Portugal and available all over the country throughout the Christmas season.

One cookie contains: *Calories:* **78** *Total Carbohydrate (g):* **7** *Sugar (g):* **2** *Carbohydrate Portions:* **0.5**
Protein (g): **2** *Fat (g):* **4.5** *Cholesterol (mg):* **11** *Fibre (g):* **2** *Glycaemic Load:* **3**

Cookies: 400 g (14 oz) sweet potatoes; 150 g (5½ oz) almonds (ground); 60 g (2½ oz) unsweetened desiccated coconut or grated fresh coconut; 1 large egg; 1 tbs runny honey; 4 tbs plain gluten-free flour; 2 tbs orange extract; 55 servings stevia

Additional: 25 g (1 oz) unsweetened desiccated coconut or grated fresh coconut; greaseproof paper

Method:
1. Pre-heat oven to gas mark 5 (190°C / 375°F).
2. Boil sweet potato (peeled and diced) on medium heat for 5-10 minutes, drain, mash, and place on low heat for 1-2 minutes to dehydrate slightly.
3. Combine the mashed potato with almonds, 60 g of desiccated coconut, egg, honey, flour, and stevia.
4. Shape the mixture into oval cookies, approx. 2.5 cm / 1 in wide (pinch the ends and flatten to make them look like leaves).
5. Sprinkle the cookies with the rest of the desiccated coconut, place on a baking tray lined with greaseproof paper, and bake for 25 minutes (or until golden brown).
6. Consume within 2-3 days (store in an air-tight container).

BANKETSTAAF (DUTCH CHRISTMAS LOG)

Total Time: 3 hours 15 minutes (preparation only: 35-40 minutes); Yield: 14 pieces

This traditional Dutch Christmas delicacy is also known as almond patties in the mid-west United States. Banketstaff consists of almond paste wrapped in pastry, and it is truly mouth-watering.

*One piece contains: Calories: **203** Total Carbohydrate (g): **13** Sugar (g): **4** Carbohydrate Portions: **1.5** Protein (g): **4** Fat (g): **16** Cholesterol (mg): **19** Fibre (g): **2** Glycaemic Load: **7***

Pastry: 125 g (4½ fl oz) self-raising gluten-free flour (chilled); 100 ml (3½ oz) coconut oil cut into small pieces (chilled); ¼ tsp fine sea salt; 75 ml (2½ fl oz) cold water

Filling: 180 g (6½ oz) almonds (ground); 1 large egg; 3 tbs runny honey; 2 tbs almond extract; 50 servings stevia

Additional: greaseproof paper; flour for rolling

Method:
1. Stir the coconut oil pieces into the flour using a round-bladed knife (ensure all the pieces are coated with flour), add water and quickly bring all the ingredients to form rough dough (still using the knife).
2. Bring the dough together with your hands and transfer it onto the work surface.
3. Without kneading, shape the dough into a wide, flat sausage, and refrigerate for 30 minutes.
4. Roll out on the dough a non-stick surface (use a dusting of flour) to a thickness of approx. 1 cm / ½ in, forming a rectangle approx. 10 x 30 cm / 4 x 12 in keeping the edges straight and the corners square (roll the dough in one direction only and be careful not to overwork the oil streaks; the pastry may be crumbly to begin with so use your hands to form the rectangle).
5. Fold the top third of the rectangle down and the bottom third up and over the top (like folding a letter).
6. Turn the dough by 90 degrees and roll out again to roughly the same size as before, then fold again and refrigerate for 15 minutes (repeat the process of rolling and folding twice more).
7. Once the pastry is ready, roll out on a sheet of greaseproof paper to form a 12 x 40 cm (5 x 16 in) rectangle.
8. Mix all the filling ingredients together to form almond paste (leave some egg for brushing) and shape into a long log (slightly shorter than 40 cm / 16 in).
9. Place the almond log on the pastry rectangle, wrap the pastry around the log (roll using the paper to assist), seal the edge (wet the edge with a pastry brush dipped in water) and pinch the ends, roll the log so that the seam is at the bottom, brush with the rest of the egg (beaten) and bake in a pre-heated oven (gas mark 5 / 190°C / 375°F) for 25 minutes (or until golden brown).
10. Once cool, cut into 14 portions (using a serrated knife), consume within 48 hours (store in an air-tight container), or freeze.

APPLE & HAZELNUT PIE

Total Time: 1 hour 55 minutes (preparation only: 45 minutes); Yield: 10 slices

---

Popular both across Europe and America apple pie is almost an essential addition to any Thanksgiving and Christmas menu, and is a great way to celebrate this delicious winter fruit. There are of course countless variations of apple pie. This one celebrates the warm spices and hazelnut, as well as the apple itself.

One slice contains: *Calories: **315** Total Carbohydrate (g): **29** Sugar (g): **12** Carbohydrate Portions: **3.5** Protein (g): **7** Fat (g): **16** Cholesterol (mg): **68** Fibre (g): **6** Glycaemic Load: **17***

Pastry: 240 g (8½ oz) self-raising gluten-free flour; 240 (8½ oz) hazelnuts (ground); 2 med eggs; 1 tbs runny honey; 4 tsp ground cinnamon; 1 tsp ground cloves; 1 tsp xanthan gum; 40 servings stevia; 15-17 tbs water

Filling: 8 med apples (approx. 750 g / 27 oz); 1 tbs runny honey; 1 med egg; 5 tsp ground cinnamon; 1 tsp ground cloves; 2 tbs pectin juice of 1 med lemon (approx. 50 ml / 2 fl oz); 30 servings stevia

Additional: sunflower oil spray, a dusting of flour (or greaseproof paper); dusting of icing sugar (optional)

Method:

1. To make pastry, combine all pastry ingredients thoroughly, knead for a few minutes (add water gradually as you may need slightly more or less, depending on the type of flour you are using), and divide the pastry in half.
2. Form one half of the pastry into a ball, roll out on a non-stick surface in a shape of a circle and transfer into a non-stick flan dish (24 cm in diameter / 9½ in) coated with sunflower spray and a dusting of flour, or lined with greaseproof paper (ensure the sides of the dish are covered with pastry and edges are smooth).
3. Prick the base with a fork and blind bake for 12-15 minutes (you can line the base with greaseproof paper and baking beans but this is not essential).
4. To make the filling, simmer apples (cored and chopped) on low heat for 20 minutes (covered) with lemon juice, honey, spices and stevia, stirring occasionally.
5. Once apple have softened, sift in pectin and continue to simmer for another 10 minutes.
6. Roll the second half of the pastry on a non-stick surface and cut out strips (width: 1-1½ cm / ½ in) using a pastry cutter or a knife.
7. Transfer the filling into the blind baked base and arrange the pastry strips on top (sticking the ends onto the base) leaving some space between them (see the photo), then arrange the second layer of pastry strips diagonally (you could weave the strips but be aware that this pastry is not very flexible so it is prone to breaking).
8. Bake for 40-45 minutes in a pre-heated oven (gas mark 5 / 190°C / 375°F) and serve warm or cold, on its own or with vanilla sauce (for recipe see GERMAN-STYLE BAKED APPLES WITH VANILLA SAUCE on page 47).
9. Consume within 2-3 days (store in an air-tight container), or freeze.

CHOCOLATE-DRIZZLED WREATH SHORTBREAD

Total Time: 50-55 minutes (preparation only: 35-40 minutes); Yield: 20 cookies

Shortbread originated in Scotland and its refinement is credited to Mary, Queen of Scots, in the 16th century. In those days, shortbread was expensive and reserved for special occasions, such as Christmas.

One cookie contains: *Calories: 102 Total Carbohydrate (g): 10 Sugar (g): 1 Carbohydrate Portions: 1 Protein (g): 1 Fat (g): 7 Cholesterol (mg): 0 Fibre (g): 0 Glycaemic Load: 7*

Shortbread: **220 g (8 oz) self-raising gluten-free flour; 120 ml (4½ fl oz) coconut oil; 1 tbs runny honey; 60 servings stevia; pinch of salt**

Chocolate drizzle: **50 ml (2 fl oz) coconut milk; 10 g (⅓ oz) cacao paste (not the same as cacao butter); 8 servings stevia**

Method:
1. Pre-heat oven to gas mark 5 (190°C / 375°F).
2. Combine all the shortbread ingredients, knead the dough for a few minutes, and then refrigerate for 10 minutes.
3. For the drizzle, combine cacao paste with coconut milk and stevia (use a glass bowl suspended over a pan with simmering water ensuring the base of the bowl does not touch the water).
4. Roll out the dough on a non-stick surface, or greaseproof paper, to a thickness of approx. ½ cm / ¼ in (use a dusting of flour).
5. Use a wide knife to help separate the cookies from the surface after they have been cut out (dough should be sufficient for twenty 7½-cm / 2-in wreath cookies).
6. Place on a non-stick tray and bake for 12 minutes (until golden brown).
7. Once cool, drizzle with chocolate topping and allow it to set.
8. Consume within 2-3 days (store in an air-tight container).

EVA'S PANETTONE

Total Time: 3 hours (preparation only: 10-15 minutes); Yield: 10 slices

Panettone is a type of sweet bread, originally from Milan, usually prepared for Christmas and New Year in Italy and other European countries, as well as across South America. Traditional panettone takes days to make. This variation is easy and quick to prepare so you can enjoy it without having to invest too much time, which is so valuable around this time of the year.

One slice contains: *Calories:* **216** *Total Carbohydrate (g):* **29** *Sugar (g):* **6** *Carbohydrate Portions:* **3** *Protein (g):* **5** *Fat (g):* **9** *Cholesterol (mg):* **91** *Fibre (g):* **1** *Glycaemic Load:* **19**

270 g (9½ oz) self-raising gluten-free flour; 4 med eggs; 60 ml (2 fl oz) coconut oil; 70 g (2½ oz) mixed dried fruit; 1 sachet fast-acting dry yeast (2 tsp / 7 g / ¼ oz); 1 tbs runny honey; 2 tbs vanilla extract; ½ tbs apple cider vinegar; 1 tsp xanthan gum (or preferred alternative); ½ tsp sea salt; 60 servings stevia; grated zest of 1 lemon; grated zest of 1 orange

Method:

1. Put the oven on the lowest setting for 10 minutes while preparing the dough.
2. Mix the dry ingredients together, add the wet ingredients (melt coconut oil on low heat first; leave a little bit of the beaten egg for brushing), and knead for a few minutes.
3. Place the dough in a non-stick baking tin (coated with oil spray and a dusting of flour), cover with cling film and leave in the warm oven to rise (turn the oven off at this point) for approximately 2 hours. The dough should have more or less doubled in size.
4. Turn the oven up to gas mark 4 (180°C / 350°F), remove the cling film, brush the dough with the rest of the egg and bake for 45 minutes, until golden-brown (insert a skewer in the centre to check the cake is cooked through; the skewer should come out clean).
5. Allow to cool and cut into 10 slices.
6. Best consume when freshly made but can be frozen or used to make PANETTONE PUDDING (to see recipe see page 57).

CASHEW & CRANBERRY FLORENTINES

Total Time: 55 minutes (preparation only: 25-30 minutes); Yield: 12 Florentines

The origin of Florentines is not clear. It appears that Florentines were most likely created in the late 17th century kitchens of French royalty. These days Florentines are still very popular all over the world, particularly during Christmas season, and their variations are countless.

One Florentine contains: *Calories:* **211** *Total Carbohydrate (g):* **18** *Sugar (g):* **11** *Carbohydrate Portions:* **2**
Protein (g): **4** *Fat (g):* **15** *Cholesterol (mg):* **0** *Fibre (g):* **2** *Glycaemic Load:* **9**

Florentines: **150 g (5½ oz) cashew nuts (roughly chopped); 100 g (3½ oz) dried cranberries; 3 tbs runny honey; 70 ml (2½ fl oz) coconut cream; 3 tbs plain gluten-free flour; 2 tbs coconut oil; 20 servings stevia**

Chocolate coating: **25 g (1 oz) cacao paste (not the same as cacao butter); 60 g (2 oz) creamed coconut (not the same as coconut cream); 60 ml (2 fl oz) coconut cream; 20 servings stevia**

Additional: **greaseproof paper**

Method:

1. Pre-heat oven to gas mark 5 (190°C / 375°F).
2. In a saucepan, mix honey, 70 ml (2 fl oz) of coconut cream, flour, coconut oil and 20 servings of stevia, and bring to the boil (stirring / whisking continuously).
3. Take off the heat and mix in nuts and cranberries.
4. Line a baking tray with greaseproof paper and using a tablespoon place the Florentine mixture on the paper forming 12 circles (leave 2½ cm / 1 in between them so they do not merge together when baking).
5. Bake for 8-10 minutes (or until golden-brown).
6. For the coating, melt cacao paste with creamed coconut and coconut milk in a glass bowl suspended over a pan with simmering water, and add stevia (do not allow the base of the bowl to touch the water).
7. Once the Florentines are completely cool, turn them upside down and spread the chocolate coating onto the base, and then refrigerate until the coating has set.
8. Keep refrigerated and consume within 3 days.

BLACK FOREST ROULADE

Total Time: 1 hour 20 minutes (preparation only: 45 minutes); Yield: 10 slices

---

Black Forest cake is believed to have originated in the late 16th century Germany, in the Black Forest (Schwarzwald) area known for the speciality liquor distilled from tart cherries (kirschwasser). Black Forest cake has gained popularity all over the world, and in many countries it remains an indulgent addition to the Christmas menu.

One slice contains: *Calories:* **214** *Total Carbohydrate (g):* **23** *Sugar (g):* **7** *Carbohydrate Portions:* **2.5**
Protein (g): **4** *Fat (g):* **12** *Cholesterol (mg):* **27** *Fibre (g):* **4** *Glycaemic Load:* **13**

Cake: **150 g (5½ oz) self-raising gluten-free flour; 1 large egg; 60 g (2 oz) creamed coconut (not the same as coconut cream); 3 tbs runny honey; 6 tbs reduced-fat cocoa powder; 50 servings stevia; ½ tsp xanthan gum**

Filling: **150 ml (5½ fl oz) coconut cream; 60 g (2 oz) creamed coconut (not the same as coconut cream); 250 g (9 oz) cherries (frozen or tinned); 1 tbs pectin; 2 tbs kirsch (optional); 10 servings stevia**

Additional: **greaseproof paper**

Method:
1. If using frozen cherries, defrost a couple of hours beforehand.
2. Pre-heat oven to gas mark 5 (190°C / 375°F).
3. Combine all the cake ingredients (chop and melt creamed coconut on low heat first), knead for a few minutes, and set aside.
4. Blend the cherries with pectin and 6 servings of stevia, add kirsch (optional) and simmer (covered) for 15-20 minutes stirring occasionally (the mixture should be quite thick).
5. Melt 60 g of chopped creamed coconut with 150 ml of coconut cream on low heat, mix in 4 servings of stevia, and set aside to cool.
6. Roll out the pastry on a sheet of greaseproof paper to form a rectangle (approx. 30 x 20 cm / 12 x 8 in).
7. Once the coconut mixture have cooled and thickened, spread it evenly onto the cake base, leaving 2 cm (approx. 1 in) off each end.
8. Apply the cherry mixture onto the coconut layer.
9. Roll slowly (the longer side) using the paper to assist, and once the roulade is formed pinch the ends to hold the filling in place.
10. Place on a non-stick baking tray and bake for 30-35 minutes.
11. Once cool, cut onto 10 slices and consume within 2 days (store in an air-tight container), or freeze.

TURRÓN DE NAVIDAD (ALMOND NOUGAT)

Total Time: 3 hours 25 minutes (preparation only: 20-25 minutes); Yield: 10 slices

Turrón, or Torró, has been known since at least the 15th century and is commonly consumed as a traditional Christmas sweet in Spain, but also in Italy, France, and some Latin American countries, as well as the Philippines.

One slice contains: Calories: **204** Total Carbohydrate (g): **14** Sugar (g): **9** Carbohydrate Portions: **1.5** Protein (g): **7** Fat (g): **15** Cholesterol (mg): **0** Fibre (g): **4** Glycaemic Load: **5**

Turrón: 300 g (11 oz) blanched almonds (roughly chopped); 5 tbs runny honey; 5 large eggs whites; 25 servings stevia

Additional: greaseproof paper

Method:
1. Place almonds on a non-stick baking tray and roast for 5-8 minutes, mixing them half way through (gas mark 5 / 190°C / 375°F).
2. Whisk the egg whites to a thick glossy meringue.
3. In a saucepan, heat up honey and bring it to a slow boil (take it off the heat once it starts to boil).
4. Gently fold the meringue into the honey and cook on low heat for 10 minutes stirring continuously (the mixture will thicken).
5. Add the roasted almonds and mix through.
6. Pour the mixture into a dish lined with greaseproof paper.
7. Place another piece of greaseproof paper directly on top of the mixture and press the mixture down.
8. Refrigerate for 3 hours before slicing.
9. Store in the fridge.

PINEAPPLE UPSIDE-DOWN CAKE

Total Time: 1 hour 15 minutes (preparation only: 25 minutes); Yield: 10 slices

---

The idea of cooking a cake upside down started centuries ago when cakes were cooked in cast iron skillets. Initially they were made with seasonal fruits, such as apples and cherries, as the canned pineapple manufacturing only began in early 1900s. This cake remains a family favourite across Europe and America all year round but it is particularly popular around holiday times.

One slice contains: *Calories:* **244** *Total Carbohydrate (g):* **32** *Sugar (g):* **11** *Carbohydrate Portions:* **3** *Protein (g):* **6** *Fat (g):* **11** *Cholesterol (mg):* **113** *Fibre (g):* **1** *Glycaemic Load:* **19**

Cake: **250 g (9 oz) self-raising gluten-free flour; 5 med eggs; 150 ml (5½ fl oz) unsweetened almond milk; 60 ml (2 fl oz) coconut oil; 1 tbs runny honey; 2 tbs vanilla extract; 1 tsp gluten-free baking powder; 50 servings stevia**

Topping: **13 pineapple slices (tinned); 12 ready-to-eat dried dates; 1 tbs coconut oil; 1 tbs runny honey; 1 tbs vanilla extract**

Additional: **sunflower oil spray; dusting of flour**

Method:
1. Pre-heat oven to gas mark 5 (190°C / 375°F).
2. In a saucepan, heat up 1 tbs of coconut oil, 1 tbs of honey and 1 tbs of vanilla extract.
3. Line a round baking tin (diameter: 24 cm / 9½ in) with parchment paper, pour the mixture in and distribute evenly.
4. Place one whole pineapple slice in the centre, and arrange the rest of the halved slices around it and around the sides, then slot small pieces of dates into the spaces (see photo).
5. For the cake, combine flour, egg yolks, almond milk, honey, coconut oil (melted on low heat), vanilla extract, baking powder, and stevia (stir or whisk until smooth but be careful not to overwork the mixture).
6. Beat egg whites (soft peaks) and gently fold into the mixture.
7. Transfer the mixture into the baking tin and bake for 50 minutes (insert a skewer in the centre to check the cake is cooked through; the skewer should come out clean).
8. Allow to cool and cut into 10 slices.
9. Consume within 2 days (store in an air-tight container), or freeze.

SALTY PISTACHIO CHOCOLATE SANDWICH

Total Time: 55 minutes (preparation only: 15 minutes); Yield: 10 slices

In culinary terms Christmas is almost synonymous with chocolate so here is another variation of a mouth-watering chocolate treat.

One slice contains: *Calories:* ***296*** *Total Carbohydrate (g):* ***9*** *Sugar (g):* ***3*** *Carbohydrate Portions:* ***1***
Protein (g): ***6*** *Fat (g):* ***27*** *Cholesterol (mg):* ***0*** *Fibre (g):* ***3*** *Glycaemic Load:* ***1***

<u>Chocolate:</u> **200 g (7 oz) creamed coconut (not the same as coconut cream); 200 g (7 oz) pistachios (ground); 5 tbs reduced-fat cocoa powder; 4 tbs almond oil; 1 tsp fine sea salt; 20 servings stevia**

<u>Additional:</u> **greaseproof paper**

Method:
1. Chop creamed coconut and melt in a saucepan on low heat.
2. Add cocoa powder, 2 tbs of almond oil and stevia, and mix thoroughly.
3. Line a non-stick bread tin, or another dish (approx. 10 x 20 cm / 4 x 8 in), with greaseproof paper.
4. Transfer half the mixture into the dish, smooth it out with a spoon, and refrigerate for 20 minutes (until completely set).
5. Combine pistachios with sea salt and 2 tbs of almond oil into a smooth paste.
6. Spread the pistachio paste onto the chocolate base evenly and cover with the rest of the chocolate paste.
7. Place another sheet of greaseproof paper on top and press down to achieve an even surface.
8. Refrigerate for further 20 minutes (until completely set), remove out of the tin, peel off the paper, and cut into 10 slices.
9. Keep refrigerated.

POLVORONES DE CANELE (CINNAMON COOKIES)

Total Time: 45 minutes (preparation only: 25 minutes); Yield: 40 mini cookies

These cookies are a popular Christmas treat in Spain, across Latin America, as well as in the Philippines.

One cookie contains: *Calories:* **49** *Total Carbohydrate (g):* **3** *Sugar (g):* **0.5** *Carbohydrate Portions:* **0.5**
Protein (g): **1** *Fat (g):* **4** *Cholesterol (mg):* **0** *Fibre (g):* **0.5** *Glycaemic Load:* **1**

125 g (4½ oz) almonds (ground); 80 g (3 oz) self-raising gluten-free flour; 100 ml (3½ fl oz) coconut oil; 1 tbs runny honey; 6 tsp ground cinnamon; 70 servings stevia; pinch of salt

Method:
1. Pre-heat oven to gas mark 5 (190°C / 375°F).
2. To make the dough, combine all the ingredients thoroughly (leaving a bit of cinnamon to sprinkle on top), knead for a few minutes, and refrigerate for 10 minutes.
3. Roll out on a non-stick surface (use a dusting of flour if required), or greaseproof paper.
4. Ideally use plunger cookie cutters or use a knife to help separate the cookies from the surface after they have been cut out (dough should be sufficient for 40 mini cookies).
5. Place on a non-stick tray and bake for 10 minutes (or until golden brown).
6. Consume within 2-3 days (keep in an air-tight container).

PECAN & VANILLA PIE

Total Time: 1 hour 30 minutes (preparation only: 30-35 minutes); Yield: 10 slices

---

Pecan pie is one of the more popular American holiday desserts. Traditionally, pecan pie contains huge quantities of syrup (sugar), which does not really fit in with the ethos of this book. But it would be a shame to miss out on it altogether so here is a variation of this pie that is delicious yet will not give you diabetes (unless you eat it all in one go that is!).

One slice contains: *Calories:* **396** *Total Carbohydrate (g):* **25** *Sugar (g):* **7** *Carbohydrate Portions:* **2.5**
Protein (g): **7** *Fat (g):* **30** *Cholesterol (mg):* **117** *Fibre (g):* **3** *Glycaemic Load:* **15**

Pastry: 200 g (7 oz) self-raising gluten-free flour; 1 large egg; 2 tbs coconut oil; 2 tbs almond oil; 1 tbs runny honey; ¼ tsp fine sea salt; 30 servings stevia; 2-3 tbs water

Filling: 200 g (7 oz) pecan nuts (ground); 4 medium eggs; 150 ml (5½ oz) coconut cream; 30 ml (1 fl oz) coconut oil; 4 tbs vanilla essence; 2 tbs runny honey; 30 servings stevia

Decoration: 50 g (2 oz) pecan nuts (halves)

Additional: sunflower oil spray; dusting of flour (or greaseproof paper)

Method:
1. Pre-heat oven to gas mark 5 (190°C / 375°F).
2. To make the pastry, combine all pastry ingredients thoroughly, knead for a few minutes (add water gradually as you may need slightly more or slightly less, depending on the type of flour you are using), and refrigerate for 10 minutes.
3. Form the pastry into a ball, roll out on a non-stick surface in a shape of a circle and transfer into a non-stick flan dish (24 cm in diameter / 9½ in) coated with sunflower spray and a dusting of flour, or lined with greaseproof paper (ensure the sides of the dish are covered with pastry and the edges are smooth).
4. Prick the base with a fork and blind bake for 12-15 minutes (you can line the base with greaseproof paper and baking beans but this is not essential).
5. To make the filling, combine all the filling ingredients, whisking or stirring (melt coconut oil on low heat first).
6. Transfer the filling into the blind baked base, decorate with pecan halves, and put back in the oven for another 40-45 minutes (check the filling has set).
7. Allow to cool and cut into 10 slices.
8. Consume within 2-3 days (keep in an air-tight container), or freeze.

RUSSIAN TEA CAKES

Total Time: 30-35 minutes (preparation only: 20-25 minutes); Yield: 18 tea cakes

Russian tea cakes are often eaten around Christmas in the United States, although variations of these cookies are also enjoyed in Mexico and a number of European countries. Interestingly, a reason for the name, or any connection to Russian cuisine, is unknown.

One tea cake contains: *Calories:* **178** *Total Carbohydrate (g):* **15** *Sugar (g):* **2** *Carbohydrate Portions:* **1.5** *Protein (g):* **4** *Fat (g):* **12** *Cholesterol (mg):* **13** *Fibre (g):* **2** *Glycaemic Load:* **8**

Ingredients: **250 g (9 oz) self-raising gluten-free flour; 200 g (7 oz) almonds (ground); 60 ml (2 fl oz) coconut oil; 40 g (1½ oz) creamed coconut; 1 med egg; 1 tbs runny honey; 1 tbs vanilla extract; ½ tsp fine sea salt; 30 g (1 oz) powdered coconut milk (not essential); 50 servings stevia; 4 tbs water**

Method:
1. Pre-heat the oven to gas mark 6 (200°C / 400°).
2. Mix flour with almonds, egg yolk, honey, coconut oil and creamed coconut (melted on low heat), vanilla, salt, stevia, and water.
3. Combine the mixture thoroughly and form into 4-cm (1½-in) balls.
4. Place on a non-stick baking tray and bake for 6-7 minutes.
5. Remove out of the oven, brush with beaten egg white, place in a bowl with powdered coconut milk and coat using a fork to roll the balls around.
6. Bake for further 3-4 minutes (if you do not wish to coat your tea cakes with powdered coconut milk, bake without removing out of the oven for 8-9 minutes).
7. Allow to cool before serving.
8. Consume within 2-3 days (store in an air-tight container).

BÛCHE DE NOËL (YULE LOG)

Total Time: 1 hour (preparation only: 35 minutes); Yield: 12 slices

---

It is thought that the first Yule log cake was probably made in the 1600s. Parisian bakers popularized it in the 19th century and nowadays this delicious dessert is traditionally served at Christmas time in France, Canada, former French colonies, and many other countries around the world.

One slice contains: *Calories:* **227** *Total Carbohydrate (g):* **19** *Sugar (g):* **6** *Carbohydrate Portions:* **2**
Protein (g): **5** *Fat (g):* **15** *Cholesterol (mg):* **38** *Fibre (g):* **2** *Glycaemic Load:* **10**

Cake: **120 g (4½ oz) self-raising gluten-free flour; 2 med eggs; 300 ml (11 fl oz) unsweetened rice milk; 100 ml (3½ fl oz) coconut milk; 2 tbs runny honey; 6 tbs reduced-fat cocoa powder; 2 tbs vanilla extract; ½ tsp xanthan gum; 30 servings stevia**

Filling: **250 ml (9 fl oz) coconut milk; 100 g (3½ oz) creamed coconut (not the same as coconut cream); 60 g (2 oz) cacao paste (not the same as cacao butter); 1 tbs runny honey; 1 tbs vanilla extract; 1 portion gelatine (for 570 ml / 19 fl oz of liquid; a vegetarian substitute can be used); 30 servings stevia; 50 ml (2 fl oz) hot water**

Additional: **dusting of icing sugar (optional); greaseproof paper**

Method:
1. Pre-heat oven to gas mark 5 (190°C / 375°F).
2. For the cake, combine all the dry ingredients, mix in all the wet ingredients and stir until smooth but be careful not to overwork the mixture.
3. Spread the mixture evenly onto a sheet of greaseproof paper placed on a flat baking tray (approx. 20 x 35 cm / 8 x 14 in) and bake for 20-25 minutes.
4. For the filling, place cacao paste, chopped creamed coconut and coconut milk in a glass bowl suspended over a pan with simmering water (ensuring the base of the bowl does not touch the water), and melt (stir continuously).
5. Dilute the gelatine in 50 ml of hot water (make sure it is completely dissolved) and add it to the cacao mixture together with honey, vanilla extract and stevia (whisk or stir until completely smooth).
6. Once cake is completely cool, peel off the paper (with paper facing up) and transfer back onto the paper.
7. Spread ¾ of the filling, which by now should be quite thick (if it is not, place in the fridge for a few minutes), onto the cake, and roll slowly (the longer side) using the paper to help.
8. Use the rest of the filling to coat the Yule log (use a fine serrated knife to achieve the log effect), and dust with icing sugar if you wish (optional).
9. Keep the Yule log refrigerated and consume within 3 days, or freeze.

CHRISTMAS PUDDING

Total Time: 6 hours 15 minutes (preparation only: 10-15 minutes); Yield: 10 slices

The origins of this pudding can be traced back to the 15th century England. At that time it was a concoction of meat, dried fruit, wine, and spices. By the 17th century meat was gone and these days the pudding is enjoyed across the United Kingdom on Christmas Day, as part of the Christmas dinner.

One slice contains: Calories: 397 Total Carbohydrate (g): 36 Sugar (g): 25 Carbohydrate Portions: 3 Protein (g): 10 Fat (g): 24 Cholesterol (mg): 106 Fibre (g): 7 Glycaemic Load: 16

Pudding: 150 g (5½ oz) mixed dried fruit; 150 g (5½ oz) ready-to-eat prunes (finely chopped); 150 g (5½ oz) almonds (ground); 100 g (3½ oz) dried cranberries; 100 g (3½ oz) walnuts (chopped); 4 large eggs; 1 Bramley apple (peeled and grated); 50 g (2 oz) milled flax seed; 1 tbs runny honey; 50 ml (2 fl oz) coconut oil (or vegetarian suet); 5 tbs brandy (optional); 4 tsp ground cinnamon; 3 tsp mixed spice; ½ tsp ground nutmeg; 50 servings stevia; grated zest of a large orange; grated zest of a large lemon; 1 tbs coconut oil for greasing

Additional: greaseproof paper; 1 tsp coconut oil for greasing; brandy for flambéing (optional)

Method:
1. If you using brandy, it is recommended to soak all the dried fruit in brandy overnight.
2. Grease your 1-L / 2-lbs pudding basin with coconut oil.
3. Combine all the pudding ingredients together thoroughly (melt coconut oil on low heat before adding), transfer into the pudding basin, press down and cover with the lid (if you do not have a lid put a sheet of greaseproof paper over it and tie with a string so that it is water / steam tight).
4. Place the basin in the pan of simmering water (coming half way up the basin) and steam for 5 hours, topping the water up periodically.
5. After 5 hours, remove the basin carefully, allow to cool, and store away or freeze (this pudding is best made up to 6 weeks in advance).
6. On the day, repeat the process steaming the pudding for another 2 hours (if frozen, allow to thaw first).
7. Once cooked, remove the pudding out of the basin turning it upside down.
8. You can flambé the pudding using brandy (optional) and serve with vanilla sauce (for recipe see GERMAN-STYLE BAKED APPLES WITH VANILLA SAUCE on page 47).

AMARETTO SWISS ROLL

Total Time: 55 minutes (preparation only: 25-30 minutes); Yield: 10 slices

Amaretto, the sweet almond-flavoured Italian liqueur, has a strong Christmas association across Europe and beyond. This cake celebrates the special amaretto flavour in a way that is both delectable and stylish.

*One slice contains: Calories: **313** Total Carbohydrate (g): **23** Sugar (g): **3** Carbohydrate Portions: **2** Protein (g): **7** Fat (g): **23** Cholesterol (mg): **38** Fibre (g): **4** Glycaemic Load: **12***

Cake: 250 g (9 oz) self-raising gluten-free flour; 60 ml (2 fl oz) coconut oil; 1 med egg; ½ tsp xanthan gum; ¼ tsp fine sea salt; 5-6 tbs water

Filling: 200 g (7 oz) almonds (roughly ground); 70 g (2½ oz) unsweetened desiccated coconut; 60 ml (2 fl oz) coconut cream; 1 med egg; 1 tbs runny honey; 1 tbs Amaretto liqueur or almond extract; 4 tsp ground cinnamon; 30 servings stevia

Additional: greaseproof paper

Method:
1. Pre-heat oven to gas mark 5 (190°C / 375°F).
2. Combine all the cake ingredients, knead for a few minutes and refrigerate for 10 minutes.
3. Combine all the filling ingredients to form smooth paste (leave some egg for brushing).
4. Roll out the pastry very thinly on a sheet of greaseproof paper to form a rectangle (approx. 25 x 35 cm / 10 x 14 in).
5. Spread the filling evenly onto the pastry base leaving 2 cm (approx. 1 in) off each end.
6. Roll slowly (the longer side) using the paper to assist, and once the roll is formed pinch the ends to hold the filling in place.
7. Place on a non-stick baking tray, brush with the remaining egg (beaten), and bake for 25-30 minutes.
8. Once cool, cut into 10 slices, consume within 2 days (store in an air-tight container), or freeze.

CHOCOLATE CHESTNUT TART

Total Time: 1 hour 30 minutes (preparation only: 30-35 minutes); Yield: 10 slices

Both chestnuts and chocolate have a strong association with Christmas so putting them together in a form of a tart is a logical thing to do. The result speaks for itself.

One slice contains: *Calories:* **284** *Total Carbohydrate (g):* **26** *Sugar (g):* **3** *Carbohydrate Portions:* **2.5** *Protein (g):* **7** *Fat (g):* **16** *Cholesterol (mg):* **106** *Fibre (g):* **2** *Glycaemic Load:* **16**

<u>**Pastry:**</u> **180 g (6½ oz) self-raising gluten-free flour; 1 large egg; 2 tbs coconut oil; 2 tbs almond oil; 2 tbs reduced-fat cocoa powder; 1 tbs runny honey; ¼ tsp fine sea salt; 30 servings stevia; 2-3 tbs water**

<u>**Filling:**</u> **180 g (6½ oz) cooked chestnuts (tinned); 170 ml (6 oz) coconut cream; 80 g (3 oz) cacao paste (not the same as cacao butter); 3 large eggs; 2 tbs brandy (optional); 1 tbs runny honey; 40 servings stevia**

<u>**Additional:**</u> **sunflower oil spray; dusting of flour (or greaseproof paper)**

Method:
1. Pre-heat oven to gas mark 5 (190°C / 375°F).
2. To make the pastry, combine all pastry ingredients thoroughly, knead for a few minutes (add water gradually as you may need slightly more or slightly less, depending on the type of flour you are using), and refrigerate for 10 minutes.
3. Form the pastry into a ball, roll out on a non-stick surface in a shape of a circle and transfer into a non-stick flan dish (24 cm in diameter / 9½ in) coated with sunflower spray and a dusting of flour, or lined with greaseproof paper (ensure the sides of the dish are covered with pastry and the edges are smooth).
4. Prick the base with a fork and blind bake for 12-15 minutes (you can line the base with greaseproof paper and baking beans but this is not essential).
5. To make the filling, blend the chestnuts and combine with all the other filling ingredients, whisking or stirring (the cacao paste needs to be melted in a glass bowl suspended over a pan with simmering water ensuring the base of the bowl does not touch the water).
6. Transfer the filling into the blind baked base and put back in the oven for another 40-45 minutes (check the filling has set).
7. Allow to cool, cut into 10 slices, consume within 2-3 days (store in an air-tight container), or freeze.

CASHEW & ALMOND AMARANTH PUDDING

Total Time: 30-35 minutes (preparation only: 5-10 minutes); Yield: 4 servings

In Scandinavia rice pudding has long been a part of Christmas tradition. This amaranth pudding is a variation of a rice pudding. It is delightfully nutty and bursting with Christmas flavours.

One serving contains: Calories: **394** Total Carbohydrate (g): **41** Sugar (g): **11** Carbohydrate Portions: **4**
Protein (g): **12** Fat (g): **23** Cholesterol (mg): **0** Fibre (g): **6** Glycaemic Load: **16**

80 g (3 oz) amaranth (can use quinoa or teff); 120 g (4½ oz) cashew nuts (ground); 60 g (2 oz) almond flakes; 1 ripe med banana; 400 ml (14½ fl oz) unsweetened almond milk; 40 g (1½ oz) mixed dried fruit; 2 tsp ground cinnamon; 1 tsp allspice; 24 servings stevia; pinch of salt; grated zest of a large orange

Method:
1. Cook amaranth as per instructions on the packaging.
2. Drain the cooked amaranth and add almond milk, mashed banana, dried fruit, spices, stevia and salt.
3. Cook on low to medium heat for 4-5 min, stirring frequently.
4. Add cashew nuts, grated orange zest and half the almond flakes.
5. Divide into 4 servings and decorate with the rest of the almond flakes.
6. Serve warm.

PISTACHIO COOKIES

Total Time: 30-35 minutes (preparation only: 20 minutes); Yield: 30 cookies

The pistachio (Pistacia Vera) is a member of the cashew family, native to the Eastern Mediterranean and Central Asia but enjoyed all over the world. Both the flavour and the colour make pistachio treats a great addition to any Christmas menu.

One cookie contains: *Calories:* **68** *Total Carbohydrate (g):* **6** *Sugar (g):* **1** *Carbohydrate Portions:* **0.5**
Protein (g): **2** *Fat (g):* **4.5** *Cholesterol (mg):* **9** *Fibre (g):* **1** *Glycaemic Load:* **3**

**200 g (7 oz) pistachio nuts (ground); 130 g (4½ oz) self-raising gluten-free flour;
30 ml (1 fl oz) coconut oil; 1 large egg; 1 tbs runny honey; ¼ tsp fine sea salt;
50 servings stevia; 2 tbs water**

Method:
1. Pre-heat oven to gas mark 5 (190°C / 375°F).
2. Combine all the ingredients thoroughly (leaving some of the egg for brushing) and knead the dough for a few minutes.
3. Roll out on a non-stick surface, or greaseproof paper, to a thickness of approx. ½ cm / ¼ in (use a dusting of flour if required as the dough will be quite sticky).
4. Use a knife to help separate the cookies from the surface after they have been cut out (dough should be sufficient for 30 medium-size cookies).
5. Place on a non-stick tray and bake for 10-12 minutes.
6. Allow to cool before serving.
7. Consume within 2-3 days (store in an air-tight container).

JAPANESE CHRISTMAS CAKE

Total Time: 1 hour 55 minutes (preparation only: 35-40 minutes); Yield: 12 slices

---

This may not be what you would expect a Japanese Christmas cake to look like but this cake is a popular choice in Japan at Christmas time. Sponge cake was popularized in Japan in the 16th century by Portuguese merchants and to this day it is celebrated by Japanese in this and various other ways.

*One slice contains: Calories: **308** Total Carbohydrate (g): **24** Sugar (g): **5** Carbohydrate Portions: **2.5** Protein (g): **8** Fat (g): **20** Cholesterol (mg): **94** Fibre (g): **2** Glycaemic Load: **15***

Cake: 270 g (9½ oz) self-raising gluten-free flour; 200 ml (7 fl oz) unsweetened almond milk; 5 med eggs; 50 ml (2 fl oz) coconut oil; 1 tbs runny honey; 4 tbs vanilla extract; 1 tsp gluten-free baking powder; 60 servings stevia

Filling: 300 ml (11 fl oz) coconut cream; 1 portion gelatine (for 570 ml / 19 fl oz of liquid; a vegan substitute can be used); 50 ml (2 fl oz) hot water; 15 servings stevia; 500 g (18 oz) strawberries (or other fruit)

Icing: 140 ml (5 fl oz) coconut cream; 100 g (3½ oz) creamed coconut (not the same as coconut cream); 5 servings stevia

Additional: sunflower oil spray; dusting of flour

Method:
1. Pre-heat oven to gas mark 5 (190°C / 375°F).
2. Combine flour, egg yolks, rice milk, honey, coconut oil (melt on low heat first), vanilla extract and stevia (stir or whisk until smooth but do to overwork the mixture), beat egg whites (soft peaks) and gently fold into the mixture.
3. Transfer the mixture into a non-stick baking tin, coated with oil spray and a dusting of flour, and bake for 55-60 minutes (insert a skewer in the centre to check the cake is cooked through; the skewer should come out clean).
4. For the filling, dilute the gelatine in 50 ml of hot water (make sure it is completely dissolved).
5. Combine the diluted gelatine with 300 ml of coconut cream and stevia (whisk for a few minutes at high speed), and allow to thicken (refrigerate for a quicker result but stir occasionally).
6. For the icing, melt chopped creamed coconut on low heat with 140 ml of coconut cream, mix in stevia, and set aside to cool.
7. Once cake is completely cool, cut it horizontally in half, spread the filling and arrange approx. 300 g (11 oz) of the strawberries (cut in half) on the bottom part of the cake.
8. Top with the second cake layer, coat with the icing, and decorate with the rest of the strawberry halves.
9. Consume within 2-3 days (keep refrigerated).

CHRISTMAS CHOCOLATE BROWNIES

Total Time: 35-40 minutes (plus decorating); Yield: 12 brownies

---

Brownies originated in the United States at the end of the 19th century and were subsequently popularized not only in the U.S. and Canada, but pretty much across the world. Brownies are loved by both children and adults and no excuse is needed to enjoy them. But if anybody needs an excuse to indulge, then Christmas seems like a good one.

*One slice contains: Calories: **396** Total Carbohydrate (g): **25** Sugar (g): **7** Carbohydrate Portions: **2.5** Protein (g): **7** Fat (g): **30** Cholesterol (mg): **117** Fibre (g): **3** Glycaemic Load: **15***

Brownies: **200 g (7 oz) self-raising gluten-free flour; 250 g (9 oz) creamed coconut (not the same as coconut cream); 150 g (5½ oz) cacao paste (not the same as cacao butter); 1 large egg; 600 ml (21½ fl oz) unsweetened rice milk; 5 tbs runny honey; 65 servings stevia**

Additional: **sunflower oil spray; dusting of flour; icing for decoration (optional)**

Method:
1. Pre-heat oven to gas mark 5 (190°C / 375°F).
2. Melt cacao paste and chopped creamed coconut in a glass bowl suspended over a pan with simmering water, ensuring the base of the bowl does not touch the water.
3. Combine with flour, egg, rice milk, honey and stevia until smooth (whisk or stir).
4. Pour mixture into moulds coated with sunflower oil spray and a dusting of flour (a single baking tray can be used).
5. Bake for 20 minutes (bake for 35-40 minutes if a single tray is used; skewer inserted in the centre should come out clean).
6. Once cool, decorate if required.
7. Consume within 2-3 days (store in an air-tight container), or freeze.

GINGER & COCONUT SWEET POTATO TARTLETS

Total Time: 1 hour 15 minutes (preparation only: 40 minutes); Yield: 8 tartlets

Sweet potato is a feature of many Christmas dishes, both savoury and sweet. This recipe provides yet another way in which this versatile and nutritious vegetable can be celebrated.

*One tartlet contains: Calories: **324** Total Carbohydrate (g): **30** Sugar (g): **5** Carbohydrate Portions: **3** Protein (g): **8** Fat (g): **20** Cholesterol (mg): **133** Fibre (g): **4** Glycaemic Load: **17***

Pastry: 170 g (6 oz) self-raising gluten-free flour; 100 g (3½ oz) unsweetened desiccated coconut; 1 large egg; 30 ml (1 fl oz) coconut oil; 1 tbs runny honey; 30 servings stevia; 5-6 tbs water

Filling: 1 med sweet potato (approx. 280 g / 10 oz); 150 ml (5½ oz) coconut cream; 3 large eggs; 5 tsp ground ginger; 2 tsp ground cinnamon; ¼ tsp ground nutmeg; ¼ tsp fine sea salt; 25 servings stevia

Additional: sunflower oil spray; dusting of flour

Method:
1. Pre-heat oven to gas mark 5 (190°C / 375°F).
2. To make the pastry, combine all pastry ingredients thoroughly, knead for a few minutes (add water gradually as you may need slightly more or slightly less, depending on the type of flour you are using), and refrigerate for 10 minutes.
3. Divide the pastry into 8 equal parts, form into balls, roll out on a non-stick surface in a shape of a circle and transfer into non-stick tartlets tins (10 cm in diameter / 4 in) coated with sunflower spray and a dusting of flour (ensure the sides of the tins are covered with pastry and the edges are smooth).
4. Prick the tartlet bases with a fork and blind bake for 15-20 minutes.
5. Peel and dice the potato, boil for 10-12 minutes on medium heat, drain and mash thoroughly.
6. Combine the mashed potato with the rest of the filling ingredients until smooth, whisking or stirring.
7. Transfer the filling into the blind baked tartlet bases and put back in the oven for another 20-25 minutes (check the filling has set).
8. Allow to cool before serving.
9. Consume within 2-3 days (store in an air-tight container), or freeze.

MARZIPAN TORTE

Total Time: 1 hour 50 minutes (preparation only: 30-35 minutes); Yield: 10 slices

---

*This torte is just another, way to enjoy almonds and cherries, two of the most popular Christmas flavours.
This dessert is light, and it is great with a cup of tea, or as a nice finish to a meal.*

*One slice contains: Calories: **340** Total Carbohydrate (g): **17** Sugar (g): **3** Carbohydrate Portions: **1.5**
Protein (g): **10** Fat (g): **27** Cholesterol (mg): **53** Fibre (g): **4** Glycaemic Load: **5***

Cake: 200 g (7 oz) almonds (ground); 50 g (2 oz) self-raising gluten-free flour; 4 med eggs;
40 g (1½ oz) almond flakes; 100 ml (3½ fl oz) unsweetened rice milk; 25 ml (1 fl oz) coconut oil;
1 tbs runny honey; 3 tbs almond extract; 40 servings stevia; pinch of salt

Filling: 400 ml (14½ fl oz) coconut cream; 500 g (18 oz) cherries (frozen or tinned); 2 portions gelatine
(each for 570 ml / 19 fl oz of liquid; a vegetarian substitute can be used); ½ med lemon (juiced);
25 servings stevia; 100 ml (3½ fl oz) hot water

Method:
1. If using frozen cherries, defrost a couple of hours beforehand.
2. Dilute one portion of gelatine in 50 ml of hot water (make sure it is completely dissolved), mix it with coconut cream and 15 servings of stevia, and refrigerate for 1 hour (stir occasionally).
3. Blend 300 g of cherries (if using tinned, drain first), mix in the second portion of gelatine (diluted in 50 ml of hot water), lemon juice, 10 servings of stevia and the rest of the cherries (whole), and refrigerate for 1 hour (stir occasionally).
4. Pre-heat oven to gas mark 5 (190°C / 375°F).
5. For the cake, combine ground almonds, flour, eggs, rice milk, coconut oil (melt on low heat first), honey, almond extract, stevia and salt, and stir until smooth but be careful not to overwork the mixture.
6. Divide the mixture into 3 equal portions.
7. Cover the bottom of a round baking tin with greaseproof paper, pour a third of the mixture in, bake for 20 minutes (or until golden brown), allow to cool, peel off the paper and set aside.
8. Repeat the process twice more and when baking the last layer, sprinkle the almond flakes on top.
9. Once the cake is completely cool, cut the layer topped with flaked almonds and one plain layer into 10 even slices (leave the bottom layer uncut).
10. Apply the cherry jelly onto the bottom layer and arrange the slices of the plain layer on top.
11. Whisk the coconut milk part of the filling for 1-2 minutes and apply onto the second cake layer, then cover with the almond flake covered slices (twist them slightly, as in the photo, to achieve a more interesting effect).
12. Keep refrigerated and consume within 2-3 days.

GERMAN-STYLE BAKED APPLES (BRATÄPFEL) WITH VANILLA SAUCE

Total Time: 50-55 minutes (preparation only: 20 minutes); Yield: 4 servings

Bratäpfel, baked apples, have been traditionally served in Germany on Nikolaus Day (Nikolaustag), December 6th.
These days they remain a popular dessert during Christmas and throughout the cold winter months.

One apple with vanilla sauce contains: Calories: 409 Total Carbohydrate (g): 35 Sugar (g): 23 Carbohydrate Portions: 3.5
Protein (g): 6 Fat (g): 29 Cholesterol (mg): 185 Fibre (g): 4 Glycaemic Load: 14

Apples: 4 medium apples; 40 g (1½ oz) chopped walnuts; 40 g (1½ oz) raisins (option: soak raisins in brandy); 1 tbs runny honey; 1 tsp ground cinnamon; 1 tsp coconut oil

Vanilla sauce: 4 med egg yolks; 400 ml (14½ fl oz) coconut milk; 2 tbs cornstarch; 2 tbs vanilla extract; 24 servings stevia

Method:
1. Pre-heat the oven to gas mark 5 (190°C / 375°F).
2. In a small bowl, mix walnuts, raisins, honey and cinnamon.
3. Remove apple cores and stuff apples with the fruit and nut mix.
4. Place the apples on a non-stick baking tin (making sure they are not touching), brush with coconut oil, cover with foil and bake for 40-45 minutes (if you like your apples crunchy, bake for 30 minutes only).
5. For the sauce, beat egg yolks with cornstarch, vanilla and stevia to a smooth paste, free from lumps.
6. Heat up the milk and slowly stir in the yolk mixture (do not boil).
7. Continue to cook on low to medium heat until the mixture thickens stirring continuously.
8. Serve apples with a warm vanilla sauce.

BASLER BRUNSLI (SWISS CHOCOLATE-ALMOND COOKIES)

Total Time: 40-45 minutes (preparation only: 20 minutes); Yield: 18 cookies

---

These chocolate-almond spiced cookies are amongst the favourite Christmas treats across Switzerland.
They are believed to have originated in the 1700s in the Basel area of Switzerland.

One cookie contains: *Calories:* **109** *Total Carbohydrate (g):* **6** *Sugar (g):* **2** *Carbohydrate Portions:* **0.5**
Protein (g): **4** *Fat (g):* **9** *Cholesterol (mg):* **0** *Fibre (g):* **2** *Glycaemic Load:* **1**

Cookies: 240 g (8½ oz) almonds (ground); 50 g (2 oz) cacao paste (not the same as cacao butter); 50 ml (2 fl oz) coconut cream; 2 med egg whites; 2 tbs runny honey; 5 tsp ground cinnamon; 1 tsp ground cloves; 1 tsp xanthan gum (or preferred alternative); 60 servings stevia

Additional: greaseproof paper

Method:
1. Pre-heat oven to gas mark 5 (190°C / 375°F).
2. Combine all the ingredients (leaving some of the egg white for brushing) and knead the dough for a few minutes.
3. Place the dough in the fridge for 15 minutes.
4. Roll out the dough on a non-stick surface or a sheet of greaseproof paper to a thickness of no more than ½ cm / ¼ in (use a dusting of flour for rolling or cover the dough with another sheet of greaseproof paper, as the dough will be very sticky). You may need to refrigerate the dough half way though if it becomes too sticky to work with.
5. Use a knife to help separate the cookies from the paper after they have been cut out (dough should be sufficient for 18 medium-size cookies).
6. Place on a non-stick tray and bake for 6-8 minutes.
7. Allow to cool before serving.
8. Consume within 2-3 days (store in an air-tight container), or freeze.

PEACH & POPPY SEED TORTE

Total Time: 2 hours 45 minutes (preparation only: 30 minutes); Yield: 10 slices

Poppy seed cakes are quite popular in Poland and other Eastern European countries, particularly at Christmas time, so here is another variation for you.

*One slice contains: Calories: **389** Total Carbohydrate (g): **33** Sugar (g): **12** Carbohydrate Portions: **3.5** Protein (g): **8** Fat (g): **25** Cholesterol (mg): **91** Fibre (g): **4** Glycaemic Load: **17***

Cake: 220 g (8 oz) self-raising gluten-free flour; 100 g (3½ oz) poppy seeds; 4 med eggs; 100 ml (3½ fl oz) unsweetened almond milk; 2 tbs runny honey; 4 tbs almond oil; 1 tsp gluten-free baking powder; 50 servings stevia

Filling: 700 g (25 oz) peach slices (tinned and drained); 200 g (7 oz) creamed coconut (not the same as coconut cream)

Additional: sunflower oil spray; dusting of flour (or greaseproof paper)

Method:
1. Soak poppy seeds in hot water for at least 1 hour (ideally overnight), wash thoroughly and drain.
2. Pre-heat oven to gas mark 5 (190°C / 375°F).
3. Combine flour, poppy seeds, egg yolks, almond milk, honey, almond oil, and stevia (stir or whisk until smooth but be careful not to overwork the mixture).
4. Beat egg whites (soft peaks) and gently fold into the mixture.
5. Transfer the mixture into a non-stick baking tin, coated with oil spray and a dusting of flour, or lined with greaseproof paper.
6. Bake for 55-60 minutes (insert a skewer in the centre to check the cake is cooked through; the skewer should come out clean).
7. For the filling, melt chopped creamed coconut on low heat, blend with 400 g (14½ oz) of peach slices until smooth, and refrigerate for 10 minutes.
8. Once cake is completely cool, cut it horizontally in half.
9. Apply half of the filling and half of the remaining peach slices to the bottom part of the cake.
10. Place the other part on top, cover with the rest of the filling and decorate with the rest of the peach slices.
11. Cut into 10 slices, consume within 2-3 days (keep refrigerated), or freeze.

SAFFRON BUNS

Total Time: 2 hours 40 minutes (preparation only: 30 minutes); Yield: 12 buns

These buns are traditionally eaten during the Christmas period across Scandinavia. They are particularly popular on Saint Lucy's Day, December 13th, when they are an integral part of the celebrations.

One bun contains: *Calories:* **214** *Total Carbohydrate (g):* **27** *Sugar (g):* **3** *Carbohydrate Portions:* **2.5**
Protein (g): **4** *Fat (g):* **10** *Cholesterol (mg):* **37** *Fibre (g):* **2** *Glycaemic Load:* **18**

Dough: **350 g (12½ oz) self-raising gluten-free flour; 150 ml (5½ fl oz) coconut milk;
70 ml (2½ fl oz) coconut oil; 30 g (1 oz) golden flax seed (milled); 3 med egg whites;
1 sachet (portion) fast-acting dry yeast (2 tsp / 7 g / ¼ oz); 1 tbs runny honey; ½ tsp fine sea salt;
½ tsp saffron threads (or a few drops of natural yellow colouring); 60 servings stevia**

Decoration: **24 raisins**

Glaze: **2 egg yolks**

Method:
1. Put the oven on the lowest setting for 10 minutes while preparing the dough.
2. Mix the dry dough ingredients together, add the wet ingredients (melt coconut oil on low heat first), combine and knead the dough for a few minutes until smooth.
3. Form the dough into a ball, place in an oven-proof dish, cover with cling film and leave in the warm oven to rise (turn the oven off at this point) for approximately 2 hours. The dough should have more or less doubled in size.
4. Remove the dough out of the oven and increase the oven temperature to gas mark 6 (200°C / 400°F).
5. Shape the dough into a log and divide into 12 equal pieces.
6. Shape each piece into a thin log (approx. 30 cm / 12 in long) and rolling each end of the log so it resembles a snail's shell aim to achieve the reverse S shape (see photo).
7. Press a raisin into each end, brush with egg yolk and place on a non-stick tray.
8. Bake in a pre-heated oven for approx. 8-10 minutes.
9. Consume within 2 days (store in an air-tight container), or freeze.

GINGERBREAD REINDEER (UPSIDE-DOWN GINGERBREAD MEN)

Total Time: 45 minutes (plus decorating); Yield: 15 reindeer

Gingerbread men were first attributed to Queen Elizabeth I, who allegedly served them to foreign dignitaries. These days, gingerbread biscuits are a popular Christmas treat across Europe and beyond. The reindeer variation is particularly enjoyed by children.

One reindeer contains: Calories: **144** Total Carbohydrate (g): **17** Sugar (g): **3** Carbohydrate Portions: **1.5**
Protein (g): **2** Fat (g): **7** Cholesterol (mg): **30** Fibre (g): **1** Glycaemic Load: **12**

Dough: 250 g (9 oz) self-raising gluten-free flour; 70 ml (2½ fl oz) coconut oil;
30 g (1 oz) creamed coconut (not the same as coconut cream); 2 med eggs; 2 tbs runny honey;
7 tsp ground ginger; 3 tsp ground cinnamon; 70 servings stevia

Additional: icing for decoration (optional)

Method:
1. Pre-heat oven to gas mark 5 (190°C / 375°F).
2. Combine all the ingredients except icing (melt coconut cream on low heat first), knead the dough for a few minutes, and then refrigerate for 10 minutes.
3. Roll out on a non-stick surface, or greaseproof paper, to a thickness of approx. ½ cm / ¼ in (use a dusting of flour if required).
4. Use a knife to help separate the cookies from the surface after they have been cut out (dough should be sufficient for 15 reindeer / gingerbread men).
5. Place on a non-stick tray and bake for 12-15 minutes (until golden brown).
6. Once cool, decorate as required.
7. Consume within 2-3 days (store in an air-tight container).

CHOCOLATE MOUSSE TORTE

Total Time: 1 hour 20 minutes (preparation only: 35-40 minutes); Yield: 12 slices

This chocolate torte is a deliciously indulgent treat. Yet another way to experience and enjoy chocolate during Christmas, or indeed any other time.

*One slice contains: Calories: **411** Total Carbohydrate (g): **23** Sugar (g): **7** Carbohydrate Portions: **2.5** Protein (g): **9** Fat (g): **30** Cholesterol (mg): **38** Fibre (g): **3** Glycaemic Load: **13***

<u>Cake:</u> 200 g (7 oz) self-raising gluten-free flour; 2 med eggs; 100 g (3½ oz) creamed coconut (not the same as coconut cream); 400 ml (14½ fl oz) unsweetened almond milk; 1 tbs runny honey; 4 tbs vanilla extract; 24 servings stevia; pinch of salt

<u>Filling:</u> 500 ml (18 fl oz) coconut cream; 200 g (7 oz) creamed coconut (not the same as coconut cream); 120 g (4½ oz) cacao paste (not the same as cacao butter); 2 tbs runny honey; 2 portions gelatine (each for 570 ml / 19 fl oz of liquid; a vegetarian substitute can be used); 2 tbs reduced-fat cocoa powder; 60 servings stevia; 150 ml (5½ fl oz) hot water

<u>Additional:</u> dusting of icing sugar and cocoa powder (optional); greaseproof paper

Method:
1. Pre-heat oven to gas mark 5 (190°C / 375°F).
2. For the cake, combine all the ingredients (chop and melt creamed coconut on low heat first), and stir until smooth but be careful not to overwork the mixture, then divide the mixture into 3 equal portions.
3. Cover the bottom of a round baking tin with greaseproof paper, pour a third of the mixture in, bake for 15-20 minutes, allow to cool and peel off the paper (repeat the process so that you have three cake layers altogether).
4. For the filling, place cacao paste and chopped creamed coconut in a glass bowl suspended over a pan with simmering water (ensuring the base of the bowl does not touch the water), and allow to melt stirring continuously.
5. Dilute the gelatine in 150 ml of hot water (make sure it is completely dissolved) and add it to the cacao mixture together with coconut milk, honey, cocoa powder and stevia.
6. Whisk for 5 minutes on high speed and set aside to allow the mixture to thicken (you may want to refrigerate it for a faster result).
7. Once the filling has set, spread half of it onto one of the cake layers.
8. Cover with another cake layer, apply the rest of the filling, place the last layer on top, and dust with some icing sugar mixed with cocoa powder (optional).
9. Cut into 12 slices, consume within 3-4 days (keep refrigerated), or freeze.

FRAGRANT FRUIT & NUT CAKE

Total Time: 55-60 minutes (preparation only: 10-15 minutes); Yield: 10 slices

Fruit cakes are served in celebration of Christmas all over the world. This particular recipe is inspired by a traditional Polish fruit cake.

*One slice contains: Calories: **320** Total Carbohydrate (g): **32** Sugar (g): **9** Carbohydrate Portions: **3** Protein (g): **9** Fat (g): **19** Cholesterol (mg): **106** Fibre (g): **2** Glycaemic Load: **18***

Cake: **200 g (7 oz) self-raising gluten-free flour; 4 large eggs; 200 ml (7 fl oz) unsweetened almond milk; 150 g (5½ oz) cashew nuts (ground); 100 g (3½ oz) walnuts (chopped); 40 g (1½ oz) mixed dried fruit; 40 g (1½ oz) dried cranberries; 2 tbs runny honey; 2 tbs coconut oil; 1 tsp gluten-free baking powder; 60 servings stevia; grated zest of two oranges**

Decoration: **5 candied cherries (optional); 1 tbs crushed almond flakes; sprinkle of icing sugar**

Additional: **sunflower oil spray; dusting of flour**

Method:
1. Pre-heat oven to gas mark 5 (190°C / 375°F).
2. Combine flour, egg yolks, almond milk, honey, dried fruit, nuts, coconut oil (melted on low heat), baking powder, stevia, and orange zest (stir or whisk until smooth but be careful not to overwork the mixture).
3. Beat egg whites (soft peaks) and gently fold into the mixture.
4. Transfer the mixture into a non-stick baking tin, coated with oil spray and a dusting of flour.
5. Bake for 45 minutes (insert a skewer in the centre to check the cake is cooked through; the skewer should come out clean).
6. Allow to cool and cut into 10 slices.
7. Consume within 2-3 days (store in an air-tight container), or freeze.

MAJA BLANCA (FILIPINO COCONUT PUDDING)

Total Time: 2 hours 15 minutes (preparation only: 15 minutes); Yield: 6 portions

This Filipino dessert is typically served during holidays, especially Christmas. The dessert is of Spanish origin, as the name "white delicacy" indicates.

One portion contains: *Calories:* **317** *Total Carbohydrate (g):* **22** *Sugar (g):* **6** *Carbohydrate Portions:* **3** *Protein (g):* **4** *Fat (g):* **24** *Cholesterol (mg):* **0** *Fibre (g):* **2** *Glycaemic Load:* **12**

400 ml (14½ fl oz) coconut milk; 300 ml (11 fl oz) coconut cream; 150 ml (5½ fl oz) unsweetened rice milk; 150 g (5½ oz) sweetcorn (tinned); 1 tbs runny honey; 50 g (2 oz) cornstarch; 25 g (1 oz) unsweetened desiccated coconut; 10 servings stevia

Method:
1. Sift cornstarch into rice milk and mix thoroughly.
2. In a saucepan, combine coconut milk, coconut cream, honey and stevia thoroughly and cook for 2 minutes on low heat.
3. Bring to the boil and slowly pour in the cornstarch mixture, stirring continuously to prevent from going lumpy.
4. Continue simmering on low heat for 4-5 minutes until the mixture is thick and smooth, stirring continuously.
5. Stir in the drained sweetcorn.
6. Pour the mixture into 6 tartlet trays (you can use one tray and portion when ready).
7. Sprinkle desiccated coconut onto a tray and place in the oven for 4-5 minutes (gas mark 5 / 190°C / 375°F, taking care not to burn it.
8. Sprinkle the toasted coconut onto the Maja Blanca, place the dessert in the fridge to allow to set for 2 hours.
9. Consume within 2-3 days (keep refrigerated).

WALNUT CAKE ROLL

Total Time: 2 hours 55 minutes (preparation only: 30 minutes); Yield: 10 slices

---

This cake is a variation of the poppy seed cake roll, and is a popular Christmas treat across Central and Eastern Europe, particularly in Hungary, Slovenia and Croatia.

One slice contains: *Calories: **319** Total Carbohydrate (g): **26** Sugar (g): **7** Carbohydrate Portions: **2.5** Protein (g): **8** Fat (g): **21** Cholesterol (mg): **106** Fibre (g): **3** Glycaemic Load: **16***

Dough: **200 g (7 oz) self-raising gluten-free flour; 50 g (2 oz) golden flax seed (milled); 3 large eggs; 60 ml (2 fl oz) coconut oil; 1 sachet (portion) fast-acting dry yeast; 1 tbs runny honey; 1 tsp xanthan gum (or preferred alternative); 30 servings stevia; pinch of salt**

Filling: **150 g (5½ oz) ground walnuts; 50 g (2 oz) mixed dried fruit; 50 ml (2 fl oz) unsweetened almond milk; 1 tbs runny honey; 1 large egg; 30 servings stevia; grated zest of 2 oranges**

Additional: greaseproof paper

Method:

1. Put the oven on the lowest setting for 10 minutes while preparing the dough.
2. Mix the dry dough ingredients together, add the wet ingredients (melt coconut oil on low heat first), combine and knead the dough for a few minutes until smooth.
3. Form the dough into a ball, place in an oven-proof dish, cover with cling film and leave in the warm oven to rise (turn the oven off at this point) for approximately 2 hours. The dough should have more or less doubled in size.
4. For the filling, combine all the filling ingredients thoroughly (separate the egg and leave the egg white for brushing).
5. Once dough has risen, roll it out on a sheet of greaseproof paper, forming a 30 x 20 cm rectangle (12 x 8 in).
6. Spread the filling evenly, leaving 2 cm (approx. 1 in) off each end.
7. Roll slowly (the longer side) using the paper to help, pinch the ends together so that no filling is visible, transfer onto a non-stick baking tray, and brush with the beaten egg white.
8. Bake in a pre-heated oven at gas mark 5 (190°C / 375°F) for approx. 30-35 minutes (until golden brown).
9. Once cool, cut into 10 slices and consume within 2-3 days (store in an air-tight container), or freeze.

ORANGE CHRISTMAS CHOCOLATES

Total Time: 30 minutes (preparation only: 10 minutes); Yield: 24 chocolates

Christmas just would not be Christmas without chocolate, especially orange-infused chocolate!

One chocolate contains: *Calories: **48** Total Carbohydrate (g): **1** Sugar (g): **0** Carbohydrate Portions: **0***
*Protein (g): **1** Fat (g): **4** Cholesterol (mg): **0** Fibre (g): **0.5** Glycaemic Load: **0.5***

100 g (3½ oz) cacao paste (not the same as cacao butter); 200 g (7 oz) creamed coconut (not the same as coconut cream); 3 tbs orange extract (oil-based); 32 servings stevia

Method:
1. Melt cacao paste with creamed coconut and stevia in a glass bowl suspended over a pan with simmering water (do not allow the base of the bowl to touch the water).
2. Add orange extract and mix thoroughly.
3. Transfer into a silicon mould and place in the freezer to set for at least 20 minutes.
4. Remove the chocolates out of the mould and serve.
5. Store in the fridge.

PANETTONE PUDDING

Total Time: 40 minutes (preparation only: 10 minutes); Yield: 6 portions

In an unlikely event of having some left-over panettone, you can use this recipe to create a delicious panettone pudding.

One portion contains: Calories: **227** Total Carbohydrate (g): **18** Sugar (g): **5** Carbohydrate Portions: **2.5**
Protein (g): **6** Fat (g): **14** Cholesterol (mg): **134** Fibre (g): **1** Glycaemic Load: **11**

**200 g (7 oz) / 3 slices panettone (for recipe see EVA'S PANETTONE on page 28);
250 ml (9 fl oz) coconut milk (or rice cream); 100 ml (3½ fl oz) rice milk original;
2 large eggs; 2 tbs vanilla extract; 1 tsp ground cinnamon; 25 servings stevia**

Method:
1. Pre-heat oven to gas mark 5 (190°C / 375°F).
2. Break up panettone slices and place them in an oven-proof dish.
3. Whisk coconut milk, rice milk, eggs, vanilla extract and stevia together.
4. Pour the mixture over the panettone.
5. Bake for 30 minutes (until golden-brown).
6. Sprinkle with cinnamon and serve warm.

DATE & MACADAMIA PINWHEEL COOKIES

Total Time: 45-50 minutes (preparation only: 25 minutes); Yield: 16 cookies

I made these cookies some years ago and they just got added to my Christmas recipes. They contain macadamia nuts and dates, plus they look festive and taste great, so definitely deserve to be on the Christmas cookie list.

One cookie contains: *Calories:* **113** *Total Carbohydrate (g):* **14** *Sugar (g):* **7** *Carbohydrate Portions:* **1.5**
Protein (g): **2** *Fat (g):* **6** *Cholesterol (mg):* **33** *Fibre (g):* **1** *Glycaemic Load:* **8**

Pastry: **125 g (4½ oz) self-raising gluten-free flour; 100 g (3½ oz) macadamia nuts (ground); 1 large egg; ½ tsp sea salt; 20 servings stevia; 3 tbs water**

Filling: **160 g (5½ oz) ready-to-eat dried dates (chopped); 1 large egg; 2 tbs water**

Additional: **greaseproof paper**

Method:
1. Pre-heat oven to gas mark 5 (190°C / 375°F).
2. Combine all the pastry ingredients thoroughly and knead the dough for a few minutes.
3. For the filling, blend the dates, egg (leave some for brushing) and water into smooth paste.
4. Roll out the pastry on a sheet of greaseproof paper to form a rectangle (approx. 15 x 40 cm / 6 x 16 in).
5. Spread the filling evenly onto the base leaving approx. 1 cm / ½ in from the long side edge.
6. Roll slowly using the paper to assist to form a 40-cm (16-in) long log.
7. Once shaped, cut into 16 pieces and place the cookies on a non-stick baking tray.
8. Flatten each cookie slightly to give it a circular shape, brush with the remaining egg and bake for 20-25 minutes.
9. Consume within 2-3 days (store in an air-tight container).

FRUITY COCONUT PUDDING

Total Time: 30 minutes (preparation time: 10 minutes); Yield: 8 portions

---

This pudding does not come from anywhere in particular (other than my kitchen), but it is yummy and very quick to make. It is an ideal treat for a cold winter afternoon, or after a nice meal.

One portion contains: Calories: **312** Total Carbohydrate (g): **31** Sugar (g): **25** Carbohydrate Portions: **3**
Protein (g): **8** Fat (g): **19** Cholesterol (mg): **133** Fibre (g): **4** Glycaemic Load: **16**

**400 ml (14½ fl oz) coconut milk; 4 large eggs; 100 g (3½ oz) almond flakes;
100 g (3½ oz) ready-to-eat dried dates; 80 g (3 oz) dried cranberries;
60 g (2 oz) ready-to-eat dried apricots; 60 g (2 oz) ready-to-eat dried mango;
2 tbs vanilla extract; 20 servings stevia**

Method:
1. Pre-heat oven to gas mark 5 (190°C / 375°F).
2. Beat eggs, and mix with coconut milk, vanilla, stevia, cranberries, and finely chopped mango, apricots and dates.
3. Divide mixture between 8 ramekins and sprinkle with almond flakes.
4. Bake for 20 minutes.
5. Serve warm.

MARZIPAN BON BONS

Total Time: 1 hour 45 minutes (preparation only: 35-40 minutes); Yield: 20 bonbons

---

There seems to be some dispute over the actual origin of marzipan. However, regardless of the origin, marzipan is an incredibly versatile confection enjoyed all over the world, particularly around Christmas time.

One bonbon contains: *Calories:* **92** *Total Carbohydrate (g):* **5** *Sugar (g):* **3** *Carbohydrate Portions:* **0.5** *Protein (g):* **3** *Fat (g):* **7** *Cholesterol (mg):* **13** *Fibre (g):* **1** *Glycaemic Load:* **1.5**

Marzipan: **200 g (7 oz) almonds (ground); 1 large egg; 3 tbs runny honey; 2 tbs almond extract; 2 tsp ground cinnamon; 50 servings stevia**

Chocolate coating: **15 g (½ oz) cacao paste (not the same as cacao butter); 60 ml (2 fl oz) coconut milk; 15 servings stevia**

Method:
1. In a saucepan, mix honey, beaten egg and stevia.
2. Heat the mixture up keeping the heat low, and stir / whisk continuously for 5-6 minutes.
3. Remove from the heat and sit in the base of the saucepan in cold water.
4. Once cool, add almond extract, cinnamon and ground almonds to the mixture.
5. Knead the mixture to form a firm paste, form into balls (3 cm / 1¼ in) and place on a baking tray or a large plate.
6. For the coating, melt cacao paste with coconut milk in a glass bowl suspended over a pan with simmering water, and add stevia (do not allow the base of the bowl to touch the water).
7. Refrigerate the chocolate sauce until it starts to thicken slightly (5-8 minutes).
8. Dip the marzipan balls in the chocolate sauce, place on a tray / plate (ensuring they do not touch), and then refrigerate until the coating has set fully.
9. Keep refrigerated.

POLISH GINGER TORTE

Total Time: 1 hour 45 minutes (preparation only: 1 hour); Yield: 10 slices

---

This cake is very popular in Poland and there are many different variations of it. Ginger cake is of course enjoyed in many other countries around the world but the particular combination of spices gives the Polish ginger cake that extra edge. Or maybe I am biased, as it reminds me of the ginger cake my grandma used to make.

One slice contains: *Calories:* **342** *Total Carbohydrate (g):* **35** *Sugar (g):* **7** *Carbohydrate Portions:* **3** *Protein (g):* **10** *Fat (g):* **19** *Cholesterol (mg):* **113** *Fibre (g):* **5** *Glycaemic Load:* **16**

Cake: **200 g (7 oz) self-raising gluten-free flour; 200 g (7 oz) almonds (ground); 5 med eggs; 200 ml (7 fl oz) orange juice; 100 ml (3½ fl oz) rice milk original; 30 ml (1 fl oz) coconut oil; 2 tbs runny honey; 1 tsp gluten-free baking powder; 5 tsp ground cinnamon; 4 tsp ground ginger; 2 tsp ground cloves; 1 tsp ground cardamom; ½ tsp ground nutmeg; ¼ tsp finely ground black pepper; 60 servings stevia; grated zest of a large orange**

Cherry jam: **500 g (18 oz) frozen cherries (take out of the freezer few hours before); 50 ml (2 fl oz) orange juice; 2 tbs pectin; 10 servings stevia**

Chocolate coating and marzipan decoration: **10 g (⅓ oz) cacao paste (not the same as cacao butter); 40 ml (1½ fl oz) coconut milk; 20 g almonds (ground); ⅓ tbs almond extract; ⅓ tbs runny honey; 24 servings stevia**

Additional: **sunflower oil spray; dusting of flour (or greaseproof paper)**

Method:
1. Pre-heat oven to gas mark 5 (190°C / 375°F).
2. Combine flour, ground almonds, egg yolks, orange juice, rice milk, honey, spices, coconut oil (melted on low heat), baking powder, stevia, and orange zest (stir or whisk until smooth but do not to overwork the mixture).
3. Beat egg whites (soft peaks), gently fold into the mixture, and transfer the mixture into a non-stick baking tin, coated with oil spray and a dusting of flour (or lined with greaseproof paper).
4. Bake for 55-60 minutes (insert a skewer in the centre to check cake is cooked; skewer should come out clean).
5. To make cherry jam, blend defrosted cherries with pectin, orange juice and 10 servings of stevia, and cook in a non-stick saucepan on low to medium heat until the mixture thickens, stirring occasionally (20-30 minutes).
6. To make the chocolate coating, melt cacao paste with coconut milk in a glass bowl suspended over a pan with simmering water (do not allow the base of the bowl to touch the water), and add 12 servings of stevia.
7. To make marzipan, combine almonds, almond extract, honey and 12 servings of stevia to form paste, roll it out on a non-stick surface, and cut out desired shapes.
8. Once completely cool, cut the cake horizontally into 3 equal slices, fill with jam, cover the cake with chocolate sauce and decorate with marzipan.

MANTECADITOS (PUERTO RICAN SHORTBREAD)

Total Time: 55-60 minutes (preparation only: 25-30 minutes); Yield: 18 cookies

These cookies are very popular during the holidays in Puerto Rico. Once you have tasted them you do understand why. They really do melt in your mouth. Delicious!

*One cookie contains: Calories: **129** Total Carbohydrate (g): **13** Sugar (g): **3** Carbohydrate Portions: **1.5** Protein (g): **1** Fat (g): **9** Cholesterol (mg): **0** Fibre (g): **1** Glycaemic Load: **8***

Shortbread: 220 g (8 oz) self-raising gluten-free flour; 150 ml (5½ fl oz) coconut oil ; 1 tbs runny honey; 1 tbs vanilla extract; pinch of salt; 40 servings stevia

Filling: 250 g (9 oz) pineapple chunks (tinned); 1 tbs pectin; 10 servings stevia

Method:
1. Pre-heat oven to gas mark 5 (190°C / 375°F).
2. Combine all the ingredients for the shortbread thoroughly (break coconut oil into small chunks) and knead the dough for a few minutes.
3. Place the dough in the fridge for 10 minutes.
4. To make the jam, blend pineapple chunks (drained) with pectin and stevia, and cook on low heat until the mixture thickens (approx. 15-20 minutes).
5. Form the dough into balls (4 cm / 1½ in), place on a non-stick baking tray, make an indent in the centre and fill with pineapple jam (leave some of the jam for brushing the cookies).
6. Brush the cookies with the remaining jam and bake for 12-15 minutes.
7. Allow to cool before serving.
8. Consume within 2-3 days (keep in an air-tight container), or freeze.

COCONUT WHITE CHOCOLATE TRUFFLES

Total Time: 45 minutes (preparation only: 15-20 minutes); Yield: 18 truffles

Yet another way to enjoy chocolate. These truffles are wonderfully indulgent and they even look Christmassy.

One truffle contains: Calories: **101** Total Carbohydrate (g): **2** Sugar (g): **1** Carbohydrate Portions: **0.2**
Protein (g): **1** Fat (g): **10** Cholesterol (mg): **0** Fibre (g): **1** Glycaemic Load: **0.2**

**140 ml (5 fl oz) coconut cream; 100 g (3½ oz) creamed coconut (not the same as coconut cream);
100 g (3½ oz) desiccated coconut; 40 g (1½ oz) cacao butter (not the same as cacao paste);
20 servings stevia**

Method:
1. Chop creamed coconut into chunks and melt it with cocoa butter and coconut cream on low heat until completely dissolved.
2. Add 80 g of desiccated coconut and stevia and mix thoroughly.
3. Refrigerate the mixture for 10-15 minutes.
4. Form into balls (3½ cm / 1½ in), coat in desiccated coconut and place on a non-stick baking tray or a large plate (ensuring they do not touch).
5. Refrigerate for further 10 minutes before serving.
6. Keep refrigerated.

PUMPKIN PIE

Total Time: 1 hour 30 minutes (preparation only: 30-35 minutes); Yield: 10 slices

---

This pie is traditionally eaten during the holidays, especially Thanksgiving and Christmas, in the United States and Canada. Even though the pumpkin is native to North America, pumpkin pie only became a common addition to the Thanksgiving and Christmas menu in the early 19th century.

One slice contains: Calories: **205** Total Carbohydrate (g): **23** Sugar (g): **4** Carbohydrate Portions: **2.5**
Protein (g): **6** Fat (g): **10** Cholesterol (mg): **117** Fibre (g): **2** Glycaemic Load: **14**

Pastry: 200 g (7 oz) self-raising gluten-free flour; 1 large egg; 2 tbs coconut oil; 2 tbs almond oil; 1 tbs runny honey; ¼ tsp sea salt; 30 servings stevia; 2-3 tbs water

Filling: 400 g (14½ oz) pumpkin puree (tinned, or boiled and mashed); 100 ml (3½ oz) coconut cream; 4 medium eggs;
1 tbs runny honey; 2 tsp ground cinnamon; 1 tsp ground ginger; ½ tsp allspice; ½ tsp ground cloves; ½ tsp ground nutmeg; 40 servings stevia

Additional: sunflower oil spray; dusting of flour (or greaseproof paper)

Method:
1. Pre-heat oven to gas mark 5 (190°C / 375°F).
2. To make the pastry, combine all pastry ingredients thoroughly, knead for a few minutes (add water gradually as you may need slightly more or slightly less, depending on the type of flour you are using), and refrigerate for 10 minutes.
3. Form the pastry into a ball, roll out on a non-stick surface in a shape of a circle and transfer into a non-stick flan dish (24 cm in diameter / 9½ in) coated with sunflower spray and a dusting of flour, or lined with greaseproof paper (ensure the sides of the dish are covered with pastry and the edges are smooth).
4. Prick the base with a fork and blind bake for 12-15 minutes (you can line the base with greaseproof paper and baking beans but this is not essential).
5. To make the filling, combine all the filling ingredients until smooth, whisking or stirring.
6. Transfer the filling into the blind baked base and put back in the oven for another 40-45 minutes (check the filling has set).
7. Allow to cool and cut into 10 slices.
8. Consume within 2 days (keep in an air-tight container), or freeze.

MINT CHOCOLATE CHRISTMAS CUPCAKES

Total Time: 35 minutes (plus decorating); Yield: 12 cupcakes

Everybody loves cupcakes so I thought it is only logical to include a cupcake recipe that can be enjoyed during the Christmas period. Mint chocolate seemed quite fitting.

One cupcake contains: *Calories:* **383** *Total Carbohydrate (g):* **28** *Sugar (g):* **8** *Carbohydrate Portions:* **3** *Protein (g):* **6** *Fat (g):* **27** *Cholesterol (mg):* **76** *Fibre (g):* **3** *Glycaemic Load:* **17**

Cupcakes: 280 g (10 oz) self-raising gluten-free flour; 4 med eggs; 5 tbs runny honey; 300 ml (11 fl oz) unsweetened almond milk; 100 ml (3½ fl oz) almond oil; 7 tbs reduced-fat cocoa powder; 4 tbs mint extract; 60 servings stevia

Icing: 240 g (8½ oz) creamed coconut (not the same as coconut cream); 240 ml (8½ fl oz) coconut milk; 4 tbs mint extract; 12 servings stevia; a few drops of natural green colouring (optional)

Additional: 12 cupcake cases (or sunflower oil spray and a dusting of flour)

Method:
1. Pre-heat oven to gas mark 5 (190°C / 375°F).
2. Combine flour, egg yolks, almond milk, honey, almond oil, cocoa powder, mint extract and stevia (stir or whisk until smooth but be careful not to overwork the mixture).
3. Beat egg whites (soft peaks) and gently fold into the mixture.
4. Transfer the mixture into 12 cupcake cases (or a non-stick cupcake tray coated with oil spray and a dusting of flour).
5. Bake for 20 minutes.
6. For the icing, place chopped creamed coconut with coconut milk in a saucepan and allow it to melt on low heat, stirring continuously.
7. Mix in mint extract, stevia, and colouring, and allow the icing to set enough to be able to pipe.
8. Once the cupcakes are completely cool, decorate with icing (you can heat the icing or cool it down to ensure the right consistency).
9. Consume within 2 days (store in an air-tight container).

MELOMAKARONA (GREEK HONEY COOKIES)

Total Time: 30-35 minutes (preparation only: 15 minutes); Yield: 15 cookies

---

These egg-shaped cookies are traditionally prepared in Greece and Cyprus during the Christmas holiday season. They are incredibly moreish.

One cookie contains: Calories: *198* Total Carbohydrate (g): *20* Sugar (g): *3* Carbohydrate Portions: *2*
Protein (g): *2* Fat (g): *12* Cholesterol (mg): *0* Fibre (g): *1* Glycaemic Load: *13*

<u>Cookies:</u> **300 g (11 oz) self-raising gluten-free flour; 170 ml (6 fl oz) olive oil;
50 ml (2 fl oz) orange juice; 2 tbs runny honey; 2 tbs brandy (optional); 1 tsp baking soda;
1 tsp gluten-free baking powder; ½ tsp xanthan gum (or preferred alternative);
50 servings stevia; grated zest of a large orange**

<u>Topping:</u> **1 tbs runny honey; 1 tbs water; 30 g (1 oz) walnuts (ground or finely chopped);
2 tsp ground cinnamon**

Method:
1. Pre-heat oven to gas mark 4 (180°C / 350°F).
2. Combine all the ingredients for the cookies thoroughly and knead the dough lightly.
3. Shape the dough into oval cookies (approx. 8 cm / 3¼ in long), place on a non-stick baking tray, and bake for 15-20 minutes (or until golden-brown).
4. Once baked and cool, place on a tray or plate, top with honey (mixed with water), and garnish with walnuts and cinnamon.
5. Consume within 2-3 days (store in an air-tight container).

TRUCHAS DE NAVIDAD (SWEET POTATO TURNOVERS)

Total Time: 1 hour (preparation only: 25-30 minutes); Yield: 14 turnovers

---

These sweet potato and almond pies are traditionally eaten in the Canary Islands during Christmas and Carnival. The name "trucha" means trout, which apparently is due to their shape. One must wonder if whoever picked the name had ever actually seen a trout, but regardless of their unfortunate name they are quite delicious.

One turnover contains: *Calories: **189** Total Carbohydrate (g): **21** Sugar (g): **2** Carbohydrate Portions: **2** Protein (g): **3** Fat (g): **10** Cholesterol (mg): **32** Fibre (g): **2** Glycaemic Load: **13***

<u>**Pastry:**</u> **270 g (9½ oz) self-raising gluten-free flour; 100 ml (3½ fl oz) coconut oil; 1 med egg; 20 servings stevia; 1 tsp xanthan gum; pinch of salt; 10 tbs of water**

<u>**Filling:**</u> **250 g (9 oz) sweet potatoes (approx. 1 med potato); 50 g (2 oz) almonds (ground); 1 med egg; 1 tbs runny honey; 3 tsp ground cinnamon; 1 tsp mixed spice; 1 tbs lemon extract (oil-based); ½ tsp anise extract; 30 servings stevia**

<u>**Additional:**</u> **dusting of flour for rolling; greaseproof paper; icing sugar (optional)**

Method:
1. Pre-heat oven to gas mark 5 (190°C / 375°F).
2. To make the pastry, combine all the pastry ingredients thoroughly, knead for a few minutes until the pastry feels smooth and elastic (add water gradually as you may need slightly more or slightly less, depending on the type of flour you are using), and refrigerate for 10 minutes.
3. Boil sweet potato (peeled and diced) on medium heat for 5-10 minutes, drain, mash, and place on low heat for 1-2 minutes to dehydrate slightly.
4. Combine the mashed potato with the rest of the filling ingredients (leave some beaten egg for brushing).
5. Roll the pastry thinly on a sheet of greaseproof paper or non-stick surface (use a dusting of flour).
6. Cut out circles using a cutter or jar (diameter of approx. 10 cm / 4 in), place a tablespoon of the filling on each pastry circle, fold the circles in half to form a half moon (press edges together with your fingers, or a fork, to seal).
7. Brush turnovers with the rest of the egg (beaten), place on a non-stick baking tray and bake for 15 minutes (or until golden brown).
8. Ideally serve warm with a dusting of icing sugar (optional).
9. Consume within 2-3 days (store in an air-tight container).

PEAR & CINNAMON CHRISTMAS TREE CAKE

Total Time: 2 hours (preparation only: 35 minutes); Yield: 15 slices

---

This cake was created simply because I could not have a Christmas cook book without a cake in a shape of Christmas tree.

One serving contains: Calories: *318* Total Carbohydrate (g): *28* Sugar (g): *8* Carbohydrate Portions: *3*
Protein (g): *6* Fat (g): *19* Cholesterol (mg): *76* Fibre (g): *4* Glycaemic Load: *16*

Cake: 370 g (13 oz) self-raising gluten-free flour; 125 g (4 ½oz) creamed coconut (not the same as coconut cream); 600 ml (21½ fl oz) unsweetened almond milk; 5 med eggs; 1 tbs runny honey; 5 tsp ground cinnamon; 1 tsp gluten-free baking powder; 60 servings stevia

Filling: 5 med ripe peeled and sliced pears (approx. 750 g / 27 oz; can use tinned but drain first); 250 g (9 oz) creamed coconut (not the same as coconut cream); 4 tsp ground cinnamon; ½ med lemon (juiced)

Additional: greaseproof paper

Method:
1. Pre-heat oven to gas mark 5 (190°C / 375°F).
2. Melt 125 g of chopped creamed coconut in saucepan on low heat and set aside.
3. In a large bowl, combine flour, 5 tsp of cinnamon, baking powder and 60 servings of stevia.
4. Add egg yolks, honey, melted coconut and almond milk, and stir until smooth (do not overwork the mixture).
5. Beat egg whites (soft peaks), add a few tablespoons to the mixture and stir, then gently fold in the rest of the beaten egg whites, ensuring the batter is smooth (the consistency should be quite thick).
6. Line baking tray(s) with greaseproof paper and spoon the mixture out to form 8 circles and a star (the diameter of the first one should be 22½ cm / 9 in, and each subsequent circle should be approx. 2½ cm / 1 in smaller than the previous one; use one baking tray for the smaller circles but ensure there is space between them to allow for the rise; use a star-shaped cutter for the star). *It is recommended to shape all the circles before putting any of them in the oven to ensure the sizes are correct and the mixture is evenly distributed.*
7. Bake the larger circles for approx. 25 minutes (or until golden brown) gradually reducing the baking time as the circles get smaller (approx. 10-15 minutes for the smaller ones; use the colour as a guide).
8. For the filling, melt 250 g of chopped creamed coconut on low heat, blend with chopped pears, 4 tsp of cinnamon and lemon juice until smooth, and refrigerate for 20-30 minutes.
9. Once cake circles are completely cool, apply the filling (it should be quite thick) shaping a Christmas tree (as in the photo), and decorate with the star.
10. Consume within 2-3 days (ideally keep refrigerated).

PANFORTE (SPICED ITALIAN FRUIT & NUT CAKE)

Total Time: 55 minutes (preparation only: 10 minutes); Yield: 16 slices

This Italian delicacy is believed to date back to the 13th century Siena. In fact, it is sometimes called Siena cake. Panforte is particularly popular in Italy during the holidays. Clearly, this version is not as sticky, as it is sugar-free, but the flavours more than make up for that.

One slice contains: Calories: *204* Total Carbohydrate (g): *20* Sugar (g): *12* Carbohydrate Portions: *2* Protein (g): *4* Fat (g): *14* Cholesterol (mg): *0* Fibre (g): *3* Glycaemic Load: *10*

Panforte: 200 g (7 oz) ready-to-eat dried dates (chopped); 100 g (3½ oz) cashew nuts ; 100 g (3½ oz) Brazil nuts; 100 g (3½ oz) hazelnuts; 100 g (3½ oz) ready-to-eat dried apricots (chopped); 80 g (3 oz) plain gluten-free flour; 40 ml (1½ fl oz) coconut oil; 30 g (1 oz) reduced-fat cocoa powder; 5 tsp ground cinnamon; 2 tsp ground cloves; 1 tsp ground cardamom; ½ tsp ground nutmeg; ½ tsp white pepper; 50 servings stevia; 100 ml water

Additional: sunflower oil spray; dusting of flour for coating; greaseproof paper; dusting of icing sugar (optional)

Method:
1. Pre-heat oven to gas mark 2 (150°C / 300°F).
2. In a bowl, mix nuts (break Brazil nuts in halves), apricots, flour, cocoa powder, spices, and stevia.
3. Blend the dates with 100 ml of water into paste, heat it up together with coconut oil, and combine thoroughly with the other ingredients.
4. Transfer the mixture into a non-stick baking tin or tray coated with oil spray and a dusting of flour (traditionally this cake is baked in a round tin), distribute evenly, top with a piece of greaseproof paper and compact the mixture your hand.
5. Remove the greaseproof paper and bake for 45 minutes.
6. Once baked, allow to cool completely and slice carefully with a serrated knife (you may want to refrigerate briefly to make sure you able to cut cleanly).
7. Dust with icing sugar (optional).
8. Consume within 3-5 days (store in an air-tight container), or freeze.

VANILLA CRESCENTS

Total Time: 40-45 minutes (preparation only: 20 minutes); Yield: 24 cookies

---

These cookies are believed to have originated in Austria but they are also traditionally eaten in other European countries during the Christmas period, including: Germany, Hungary, Czech Republic, Slovakia, and Romania.

*One cookie contains: Calories: **72** Total Carbohydrate (g): **6** Sugar (g): **1** Carbohydrate Portions: **3** Protein (g): **1** Fat (g): **5** Cholesterol (mg): **9** Fibre (g): **1** Glycaemic Load: **4***

Dough: 140 g (5 oz) self-raising gluten-free flour; 60 g (2 oz) almonds (ground); 80 ml (3 fl oz) coconut oil; 1 tbs runny honey; 4 tbs vanilla extract; 1 med egg; 60 servings stevia

Additional: icing sugar for dusting (optional)

Method:
1. Pre-heat oven to gas mark 5 (190°C / 375°F).
2. Combine all the ingredients thoroughly, knead for a few minutes, and refrigerate for 10 minutes.
3. Form dough into crescents (see photo) and place on a non-stick baking tray.
4. Bake for 12-15 minutes (until golden brown).
5. Once baked, dust with icing sugar (optional).
6. Consume within 2-3 days (store in an air-tight container), or freeze.

About the author

I started my therapy training 16 years ago. Over the years, I have worked with a wide range of clients, both in the UK and abroad. I have successfully supported people with weight problems, depression, anxiety, chronic pain, compromised immune function, as well as digestive, skin and cardiovascular conditions. My training in the field of human physiology and nutritional sciences includes a doctorate degree in Physiology, Biochemistry and Nutrition, as well as a Master of Science degree in Human Nutrition. I am also trained in clinical and medical hypnotherapy, and I am a Master Practitioner of Neuro-Linguistic Psychology.

Due to my own dietary restrictions, I have a particular interest in providing support for people with special dietary requirements, and I am extremely passionate about creating wheat, gluten, dairy and refined sugar-free food that is delicious, healthy, and looks amazing.

For more information and resources, visit:
www.dr-eva.com

To join my gluten & dairy-free facebook community, go to:
www.facebook.com/yummyfreefromrecipes

If you like this book, you may want to have a look at my previous book:
Easy-to-follow Wheat, Gluten & Dairy-free Recipes. Weight Loss & Diabetes Friendly.

This book offers 110 wheat, gluten, dairy and refined-sugar-free recipe ideas that are bursting with flavour and are easy to follow (plus 20 easy snack ideas). The recipes are designed to help optimise blood sugar control, and are therefore suitable for people with diabetes and those wanting to lose weight. Each recipe is accompanied by a comprehensive nutritional analysis and a photo of a finished product. The well-researched introductory section contains a wealth of information about healthy wheat, gluten and dairy-free living, as well as an extensive list of invaluable weight loss tips. This book is suitable for both novice and experienced cooks. The recipes are inspired by Mediterranean, Eastern European and Asian cuisine.

For more information, or to buy, go to:
www.dr-eva.com/new-cook-book

Printed in Great Britain
by Amazon.co.uk, Ltd.,
Marston Gate.